A Glossary of Rhetorical Terms

Second Edition

By Gregory T Howard

To order additional copies of this book, contact:
Xlibris
1-888-795-4274
www.Xlibris.com
Orders@Xlibris.com
777790

"(Rhetorical figures) should be unseen, for the sublimity of the whole should overshadow the minute details used…a powerful effect usually attends the union of figures for a common object, when two or three mingle together as it were in partnership, and contribute a fund of strength, persuasiveness, and beauty."

Longinus, *On the Sublime*

To my **father,**
whose passion for communication
fuels my desire to make it more precise

Contents

A Note on the Second Edition

Every writer desires to write more effectively, every speaker wishes to deliver more powerful orations, and every person wants to communicate more clearly. Those who achieve clarity and effectiveness usually stumble upon it eventually over many years of practice and repetition. Rhetoric makes this process more efficient and effective by providing writers or speakers with the tools to analyze and improve upon their own formal communication. This resource contains over 400 rhetorical devices and definitions. These devices are the music notes of communication. Their study and proper use allow individuals to intricately orchestrate their thoughts and ideas into clear and beautiful statements, sentences, and speeches.

The focus of the First Edition of this resource was too broad. At that time, it was my goal to include everything in a single volume, and though that was helpful in some ways, it also detracted from the main reason I wanted to compile and publish a glossary like this in the first place. I have, in this Second Edition, rectified that mistake. This edition is condensed and streamlined for students of rhetoric and communication as they analyze, imitate, and invent. This glossary was specifically created to aid one with Rhetorical Coding, a method of speech analysis that is meant to encourage analysis, imitation, and ultimately invention. A full explanation of this method can be found in my book: *Rhetorical Coding: Analyze, Imitate, Invent.*

Sample Gloss:

Accumulatio

Bringing together various points made throughout a speech and presenting them again in a climactic way.

RC: **A5** ◀——— *Rhetorical Coding Number*

Example: *This sentence comes after a lengthy passage in which Churchill warns the public that their courage and effort are still needed to defeat the enemy*: "Your organization, your vigilance, your devotion to duty, your zeal for the cause must be raised to the highest intensity." - Winston Churchill, Speech, 14 July 1941.

Notes: *none.*

The sample gloss above contains several parts, including the Rhetorical device, figure, or term, the definition, a **Rhetorical Coding Number**, an example of how the device might be used in literature or in speech, and any specific or interesting notes about the device. Most of this can be found in any of the various Rhetorical handlists or glossaries at your local bookstore, but what you will not find anywhere else is a number associated with each device. This number is its Rhetorical Coding Number, which provides someone interested in analyzing formal speech a means by which to do so. Along with this addition, a short list of the most popular devices and their numbers can be found in **Appendix A** of this glossary.

A

Abate
English synonym of Anesis.

Abbaser
English synonym of Tapinosis.

Abecedarian
An Acrostic whose letters do not spell a word but follow alphabetical order.
RC: **A1**
Example: **A**lone **B**ehind **C**losed **D**oors.

Notes: The use of this device in writing or oratory is limited mainly to the realm of memorization. It is a form of composition that allows the audience to recall, without much difficulty, previous points or points after the fact.

Ablatio
Latin synonym of Aphaeresis.

Abode
English synonym for Commoratio.

Abominatio
Expressing hatred toward or for a person, place, or thing.
RC: **A2**
Example: "…and I re-tell thee again and again, **I hate the Moor**…" – Shakespeare, *Othello Act III Scene I*

Notes: Abominatio is a Latin synonym of Bdelygmia and Apodixis and a stronger form of Exouthenismos.

Abscisio
Latin synonym of Apocope.

Abuse
The use of a word in a context that differs from its proper usage.
RC: **A3**
Example: Staying up all night, we were able to witness the *birth of the sun*.
(In the example sentence the rise of the sun is said to be its birth, and though we know what is meant, it is a misapplication of the term. Birth refers to either child bearing or the bringing of something into existence, and since the sun is doing neither it is considered an abuse of the word.)

Notes: Due to its nature, this device is often the enemy of precision; however, it can result in powerful imagery.

Abusio
Latin synonym for Catachresis.

Abusion
English synonym for Catachresis.

Accismus
A fabricated and insincere refusal of that which is very much desired.
RC: **A4**
Example: *Said in a halfhearted way*: Oh, you shouldn't have.

Accumulatio
Bringing together various points made throughout a speech and presenting them again in a climactic way.
RC: **A5**

Example: *This sentence comes after a lengthy passage in which Churchill warns the public that their courage and effort are still needed to defeat the enemy:* "Your organization, your vigilance, your devotion to duty, your zeal for the cause must be raised to the highest intensity." - Winston Churchill

Acoloutha

Substituting one word with another whose meaning is very close to the original, but one could not use the original word as the substitute for the second.

RC: **A6**

Example: Grant is an incredibly smooth guy; his cunning is all but invisible to those who encounter it. *(In the second clause the word "cunning" replaces the word "smooth." This replacement is not reciprocal; "cunning" would usually not replace the word "smooth." For example, no one would call a "smooth" rock "cunning.")*

Notes: Acoloutha is related to but not exactly a Synonym.

Acrostic

When the first letters of progressive lines are arranged in alphabetical order are used to spell a word.

RC: **A7**

Example: The 5 points of Calvinism.

> **T**otal depravity
> **U**nconditional election
> **L**imited atonement
> **I**rresistible grace
> **P**erseverance of the saints

Notes: The use of this device in writing or oratory is limited mainly to the realm of memorization. It is a form of composition that allows the audience to recall without much difficulty previous points or points after the fact.

Acyrologia

An incorrect use of words, especially the use of words that sound alike but are far in meaning from the speaker's intentions.

RC: **A8**

Notes: Related in effect, but different in motive from Abuse. See Abuse.

Acyron

The use of a word or phrase which is contrary to what is meant.

RC: **A9**

Example: "Never could I have hoped for such great woe." —*Aeneid 4.419*

Adage

One of several terms describing short, pithy sayings, or traditional expressions of conventional wisdom.

RC: **A10**

Example: The early bird gets the worm.

Notes: **Types of Adage:**
1. **Aphorism:** A pithy expression which has not necessarily gained credit through long use but which is distinguished by particular depth or good style.
2. **Cliché**: An overused adage.
3. **Epigram:** An adage that is distinguished by wit or irony.
4. **Gnome:** A short pithy saying that expresses a general idea or principle.
5. **Maxim:** A general rule of conduct – usually contains a call to action.
6. **Paroemia**: A short pithy saying.
7. **Proverb:** Products of folk wisdom which attempt to summarize some basic truth.
8. **Sententia**: A short pithy saying used as a summary of what has previously been said.

Adhortatio

A commandment, promise, or exhortation intended to move one's consent or desires.

RC: **A11**

Example: "...but showing steadfast love to thousands of those who love me and keep my commandments. You shall not take the name of the LORD your God in vain, for the LORD will not hold him guiltless who takes his name in vain." - Exodus 20:6-7 ESV

Adianoeta

To convey a surface level meaning, while at the same time including or conveying a deeper second meaning.

RC: **A12**

Admittance
See Paromologia

Adnominatio
Assigning to a proper name its literal or homophonic meaning.
RC: **A13**
Example: **Mr. Baker** must be the best **bread maker** around.

Notes: The word derives from the Latin *nominare*, meaning to name.

Adynata
A declaration of impossibility or perhaps an expression of the impossibility of expression.
RC: **A14**
Example: "Again I tell you, it is easier for a camel to go through the eye of a needle than for a rich person to enter the kingdom of God." - Matthew 19:24 ESV

Aetiologia
A figure of reasoning by which one attributes a cause for a statement or claim made, often as a simple relative clause of explanation.
RC: **A15**
Example: "So I am eager to preach the gospel to you also who are in Rome. For I am not ashamed of the gospel, for it is the power of God for salvation to everyone who believes, to the Jew first and also to the Greek." — Romans 1:15-16 ESV

Affirmatio
Stating something as though it had been in dispute or in answer to a question, though it has not been.
RC: **A16**

Notes: Affirmatio can be used to avoid argumentation or challenge after a point is delivered. It is not only a strong device of Logos, but it can also be a strong device of Ethos as well.

Aganactesis

A proclamation of conscious hate.

RC: **A17**

Example: You are incredibly stupid – foolish, idiotic – stupid!

Notes: Aganactesis is usually an expression which occurs in the form of an outburst (whether it is provoked or not).

Agnominatio

The repetition of a word, changing it in letter or sound.

RC: **A18**

Example: We call it a **creek**, but if you're from Southern Pennsylvania you may say **crick**.

Allegory

A sustained Metaphor continued through whole sentences or even through a whole discourse.

RC: **A19**

Example: The most obvious use of allegory is found in work-length narratives such as Bunyan's *Pilgrim's Progress* or Dante's *Inferno*.

Notes: Allegory is characterized by occurring without any introduction or explanation. It is a device which relies on the audience's ability to suspend their disbelief. Although it is related to Conceit it is quite different. Conceit deals with a picture that has two different levels of meaning. An Allegory also has two levels of meaning but deals with symbols or types.

Alliteration

Repetition of the same letter or sound within nearby words.

RC: **A20**

Example: The star slipped silently out of sight.

Notes: A device commonly used in poetry. Kinds of Alliteration include: Assonance, Consonance, and Paroemion.

Allotheta

Substitution of one case, gender, mood, number, tense, or person for another.

RC: **A21**

Example: When **he** wore a dress, **she** looks delightfully female. (Through Allotheta the word "she" has been substituted for the pronoun "he.")

Notes: A synonym of <u>Enallage</u>.

Ambage, *figure of*

Supplying a descriptive phrase in place of a name.

RC: **A22**

Example: Your **couch potato** of a father was far too lazy to mow the lawn today.

Ambiguitas

Ambiguity of grammatical structure often resulting in or created by incorrect punctuation. (general ambiguity)

RC: **A23**

Amphibologia/ambiguous: An overarching term for that which is unclear – usually resulting in misunderstanding.

RC: **A24**

Ampliatio

Using the name of something or someone before it has obtained that name or after the reason for that name has ceased.

RC: **A25**

Example: A good example of this can be found in John Milton's Paradise Lost, where the author calls upon a muse to teach him the names of the satanic generals in hell whose names are not known until much later.

Notes: A form of Epitheton.

Anacoenosis

Asking the opinion or judgment of the judges or audience.

RC: **A26**

Example: "Did this in Caesar seem ambitious? When that the poor have cried, Caesar hath wept: Ambition should be made of sterner stuff: yet Brutus says he was ambitious; And Brutus is an honourable man. You all did see that on the

Lupercal I thrice presented him a kingly crown, which he did thrice refuse: was this ambition?" – Shakespeare, *Julius Caesar Act II Scene III*

Anacoluthon
A failure to follow on; a departure from the grammatical scheme of a given sentence.
RC: **A27**
Example: What could you or would you...for you were not there.

Anadiplosis
The repetition of the last word (or phrase) from the previous line, clause, or sentence at the beginning of the next.
RC: **A28**
Example: "Men in great place are thrice **servants**: **servants** of the sovereign or state; **servants** of fame; and **servants** of business." – Francis Bacon

Analogy
A comparison drawn from like figures between two different things.
RC: **A29**

Notes: **Kinds of Analogy**
General Analogy – An analogy that is not specific to either the listener or the speaker, but instead derives its comparison from common knowledge.
Disconnected Analogy – An analogy that either applies or comes from the experience or knowledge of either the listener or the speaker, but not both at the same time.
Common Analogy – An analogy that has been experienced or is known by both the speaker and the listener.

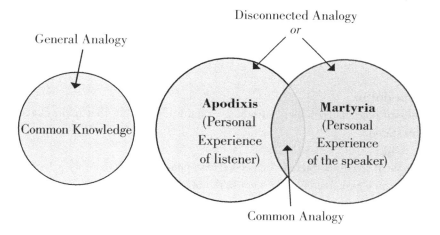

Anamnesis
Calling to memory past matters. More specifically, citing a past author from memory.
RC: **A30**

Notes: This device traditionally focuses on sad memories of the past and is found in eulogies.

Anangeon
Arguing on the basis of inevitability or necessity.
RC: **A31**
Example: I know it looks bad, but I killed him purely out of self-defense.

Notes: This device is customarily used in a Judicial Oratory. See Oration.

Anaphora
Repetition of the same word or group of words at the beginning of neighboring clauses, sentences, or lines – granting emphasis to a particular phrase or word.
RC: **A32**
Example: "**We shall** not flag or fail. **We shall** go on to the end. **We shall** fight in France, **we shall** fight on the seas and oceans, **we shall** fight with growing confidence and growing strength in the air, **we shall** defend our island, whatever the cost may be, **we shall** fight on the beaches, **we shall** fight on the landing grounds…" — Winston Churchill

Notes: The most effective use of this device is found in conjunction with parallel clauses.

Anapodoton
A subordinate clause which introduces a main clause, but that main clause is never stated.
RC: **A33**
Example: If you think you have succeeded in stopping me... (Here we see a dependent clause which grammatically does not work but still makes sense.)

Notes: An elongated form of Ellipsis.

Anastrophe
Departing from normal or natural order in a sentence for the sake of emphasis.
RC: **A34**

Anemographia
A good and vivid description of wind – usually in an attempt to create a sense of reality.
RC: **A35**
Example: The wind rushed and swirled around the room throwing the leaves of paper parading across the room. It hummed through the windows and exhaled up the chimney. It was all I could do to stand still in its vicious currents.

Anesis
Adding a concluding sentence or phrase that diminishes the effect of what has been said previously.
RC: **A36**
Example: Dylan was a promising student. He maintained a 4.0 throughout high school and college, knew exactly where he was heading in life, and had married an equally brilliant girl, *but that was before the accident.*

Notes: Anesis is often seen as the opposite of Epitasis. This device is often used to create irony, sarcasm, or a paradox.

Antanaclasis

The repetition of a word or phrase but the meaning of the word changes the second time it is used.

RC: **A37**

Example: "Your argument is sound...all sound." - Benjamin Franklin

Notes: Antanaclasis in closely related to the English pun and is a Figure of Repetition. Its use is quite limited, by its very nature, in both written and oral communication. See Figures of Repetition.

Antanagoge

Acknowledging something to be difficult or negative but putting a positive spin on it.

RC: **A38**

Example: "When life gives you lemons, make lemonade." – Elbert Hubbard

Antapodosis

A kind of Simile in which many factors or attributes are comparable.

Anthimeria

Substitution of one part of speech for another (participle is an example).

RC: **A39**

Example: Irving Babbitt warned us that colleges have become too **democratized.** (Noun used as a verb)

Anthropopatheia

Ascribing human attributes or characteristics to non-human creatures, beings, or concepts - usually attributes of humans used to describe God.

RC: **A40**

Example: "Being therefore exalted at the right **hand of God** and having received from the Father the promise of the Holy Spirit, he has poured out this that you yourselves are seeing and hearing." - Acts 2:33 ESV

Notes: This becomes quite useful when a being or object is far beyond the ability of human comprehension. However, this device should not be overused.

According to Irving Babbitt the dehumanization of man by this and other related devices will lead ultimately to a destructive movement.

Anthypophora
Reasoning done by asking oneself questions and then immediately answering them.
RC: **A41**
Example: Is the Democratic Party the best? I think not. Why else were they beaten? Because they no longer know what the people want.

Notes: A figure of reasoning generally used to create a desired effect. It is usually employed to overwhelm the hearers, in which case the questions are difficult to answer. It is often employed, as all Figures of Questioning, as a means of appearing, for a time, as a neutral party. See Figures of Questioning.

Anticategoria
A retort in which one turns the very accusation made by one's adversary back against him.
RC: **A42**
Example: Compared to you, I am no drunkard.

Antilogy
A contradiction either in terms or ideas. Antilogy can often refer to two speeches which are in opposition — whether by accident or in debate.

Antimetabole
Repetition of words, in successive clauses, in reverse grammatical order.
RC: **A43**
Example: "Ask not what your country can do for you; ask what you can do for your country."
— John F. Kennedy, *Inauguration Speech*

Notes: This device holds much of the same effect as other Figures of Repetition, but it lacks the strong Appeal to Pathos, because of its slightly hidden nature. When used in written form it becomes much clearer and can be identified and appreciated as artful. The identification of this device, however, is not its entire power. See Figures of Repetition.

Antiphrasis
Irony of one word, often derisively, through obvious contradiction.
RC: **A44**
Example: Oh yes, you are awfully **fat**! (Said of a **skinny** individual.)

Notes: Antiphrasis is a synonym of Paralipsis and a type of Irony. See Irony.

Antiprosopopoeia
Using inanimate objects to represent humans.
RC: **A45**
Example: (In the following poetic lines, the cloud and the daffodils both refer to human beings)

"I wandered lonely as a cloud
That floats on high o'er vales and hills,
When all at once I saw a crowd,
A host of golden daffodils…" – William Wadsworth, *Daffodils*

Notes: "Antiprosopopoeia comes from the Greek. Anti, meaning: 'opposite,' prosopon meaning 'face' or 'person', and poiein, meaning 'to make'. See also Personification, and its opposite Prosopopoeia."[1]

Antiptosis
One grammatical case is substituted for another.
RC: **A46**
Example: Me want candy, instead of, I want candy.

Antirrhesis
Rudely rejecting the opinion or authority of someone.
RC: **A47**

---

[1]   From Gideon Burton's *Silva Rhetoricae* at humanities.byu.edu/rhetoric/Silva.htm

Notes: Antirrhesis comes from a Greek word that means 'refutation' or 'counter-statement.'[2]

Antisagoge
Producing a hypothetical situation or a precept to illustrate opposing and alternative consequences – usually dealing with reward and punishment.
RC: **A48**
Example: "See, I have set before you today life and good, death and evil. 16 If you obey the commandments of the LORD your God that I command you today, by loving the LORD your God, by walking in his ways, and by keeping his commandments and his statutes and his rules, then you shall live and multiply, and the LORD your God will bless you in the land that you are entering to take possession of it. 17 But if your heart turns away, and you will not hear, but are drawn away to worship other gods and serve them, 18 I declare to you today, that you shall surely perish. You shall not live long in the land that you are going over the Jordan to enter and possess…" —Deuteronomy 30:15-18 ESV

Antistasis
The repetition of a word in a different or contrary sense.
RC: **A49**
Example: "He that composes himself is wiser than he that composes a book." – Benjamin Franklin

Antisthecon
The substitution of a letter in a word for another letter to create irony.
RC: **A50**

Antithesis
Juxtaposition of contrasting words or ideas.
RC: **A51**
Example: "It has been my experience that folks who have no vices have very few virtues."
– Abraham Lincoln

---

[2]   Ibid.

Notes: Antithesis is the grammatical form of Antitheton. Antitheton deals with contrasting thoughts or proofs in an argument; Antithesis deals with contrasting words or ideas within a phrase, sentence, or paragraph.

Antitheton

A proof or composition constructed of contraries.

RC: **A52**

Example: "It was the **best of times**; it was the **worst of times**." – Charles Dickens, *Tale of Two Cities*

Notes: See Antithesis.

Antonomasia

Substituting a descriptive phrase for a proper name, or substituting a proper name for a quality associated with it.

RC: **A53**

Example: Yes, The Bard did write "The Scottish Play." ("The Bard" replaces "Shakespeare" and "The Scottish Play" replaces Macbeth)

Apaetesis

An argument which, because of anger, is set aside until the anger subsides.

Apagoresis

A statement designed to inhibit someone's actions or desires.

RC: **A54**

Example: If you carry on in this manner I will never talk to you again.

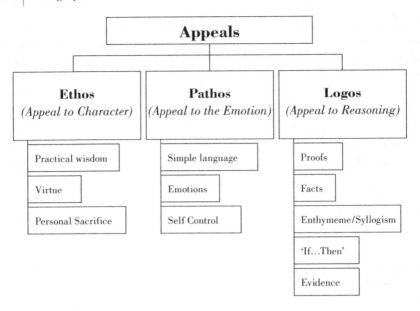

Appeal
A persuasive plea or specifically aimed proof.

Notes: See also Ethos, Pathos, and Logos. The Art of Rhetoric is concerned with the three persuasive appeals (Logos, Pathos, Ethos) and their proper mixture. Aristotle, in his work on Rhetoric, says that Rhetoric is concerned with these types of pleas and proofs because, unlike contracts and strict evidence, they deal in the art of persuasion.

Aphaeresis
The omission of a syllable or letter at the beginning of a word.
RC: **A55**
Example: "The King hath cause to **plain**." ('Plain' replaces 'complain')—Shakespeare, King Lear Act III Scene I

Notes: Aphaeresis is a type of Metaplasm, and therefore, it is used to keep meter or rhyme in a piece. See Metaplasm.

Aphorismus
Calling into question the proper use of a word.

RC: **A56**

> Example: "For you have but mistook me all this while.
> I live with bread like you, feel want,
> Taste grief, need friends: subjected thus,
> How can you say to me I am a king?"—Shakespeare, Richard II

Notes: Aphorismus will often be used in question form. It is a figure which contrasts a specific instance. It is dependent upon the present subject matter and the ordinary definition of a word or idea. For instance, in the example above Richard II calls into question the title King, not because he does not have that official title upon him, but because he questions the implications or necessary traits seemingly required for such a title.

Apocarteresis

Casting of all hope away from one thing and placing it on another source altogether.
RC: **A57**
Example: "In his name the gentiles will hope." – Matthew 12:21 ESV

Notes: Apocarteresis, if used correctly, is one of the strongest coalition of Appeals – mainly Ethos and Pathos. This figure's effectiveness will be totally based upon the likeness of aims between the audience and the speaker.

Apocarteresis Syncrisis:

Juxtaposing, by Syncrisis, the fact that you cannot accomplish the said goal or problem, but someone else can. Its specific pattern is: Apodixis into Syncrisis into Anamnesis.
RC: **A58**
Example: "You can't bring men back from the dead, but God did."

Notes: Apocarteresis is a Rhetorical pattern (a mix of several devices to achieve a particular effect or more holistic Appeal [See Appeal]) which uses the past to prove your inability to tackle something in the present. Although Anamnesis is suggested, it could be possible to use Epicrisis in its place. It also is more appealing and effective if a Figure of Repetition or Parallelism is employed.

Apocope

Omitting a letter or syllable at the end of a word.

RC: **A59**
Example: Shakespeare so **oft'** made use of Apocope in his plays.

Notes: Apocope is a type of Metaplasm, and therefore, it is used to keep meter or rhyme in a piece. See Metaplasm.

Apodioxis
The strong rejection of something or someone as being rude, unnecessary, absurd, false, or evil.
RC: **A60**
Example: "No, Mister President, you are not protecting women, you are authorizing the destruction of 500,000 thousand little women every year. No, Mr. President, you are not protecting reproductive freedom, you are authorizing the destruction of freedom for 1,000,000 little human beings every year. No, Mr. President, killing our children is killing our children no matter how many times you say it is a private family matter..." – John Piper, *Response to President Obama*

Notes: The strength of Apodioxis is quite clear, but it must be incorporated correctly. The user will find a more complete effect if they place this deice in close proximity to figures of praise. If one attribute of the idea or person presented is praised and then another rejected by Apodioxis the argument becomes more appealing. For example: when John Piper rejects the President's decision concerning abortion he begins by telling how he wept for joy at his election. This places him as a caring individual who others can easily relate to.

Apodixis
Proving a statement by referring to common knowledge or general experience.
RC: **A61**
Example: Everyone knows that it takes about seven years to digest gum.

Notes: Common knowledge is an interesting phenomenon, for it centers around something that everyone knows. This requires a relative perspective. This device becomes a lot less effective if you are outside of your normal environment or culture. Therefore, the use of Apodixis should be limited to your personal sphere of knowledge (i.e. your country, your workplace, your home...etc.). The assertion that something is "common knowledge" is sometimes associated with the fallacy argumentum ad populum (Latin: "appeal to the people"). Misinformation is easily introduced into rumors by intermediate messengers. In many cases "common knowledge" is also widely established as being true. So then the assertion that something is "common knowledge," is merely another way of saying that someone is ignoring an obvious fact, or should have known about it had they been paying attention.

Apologue
Appeasing and persuading the rude and ignorant through fable type comparisons.
RC: **A62**

Apophasis
Raising a point or idea without really raising it.
RC: **A63**

Notes: Related terms include: Cataphasis, Paralipsis, Praeteritio.

Apoplanesis
Promising to address the issue but effectively dodging it through deviation.
RC: **A64**
Example: You all have been asking about my stance on this war, and I will answer. In fact, all these questions you have been asking have been good, to the point, and really give me an opportunity to address the pressing issues facing our great nation.

Notes: From the Greek word meaning to "lead astray".[3] Apoplanesis is a device made popular in the political realm. However, it does have merit when there is very little to say in approval of a certain point or argument.

Aporia
Deliberating, in doubt, with oneself and/or asking oneself what the best or most appropriate way is to approach something.
RC: **A65**
Example: "I am at no loss for information about you and your family; but I am at a loss where to begin. Shall I relate how your father Tromes was a slave in the house of Elpias, who kept an elementary school near the Temple of Theseus, and

---

[3]   See Gideon Burton's *Silva Rhetoricae* at humanities.byu.edu/rhetoric/Silva.htm on the word Apoplanesis.

how he wore shackles on his legs and a timber collar round his neck? or how your mother practised daylight nuptials in an outhouse next door to Heros the bone-setter, and so brought you up to act in tableaux vivants and to excel in minor parts on the stage?" – Demosthenes, *On the Crown*[4]

Notes: In the realm of philosophy an Aporia is a puzzle or a seemingly unsolvable point in a discussion, often arising as a result of two equally plausible yet inconsistent premises. Aporia can be seen best in the early Greek dialogues where Aristotle, Plato, and Socrates argue points by questioning their validity. See Figures of Questioning.

Aposiopesis

Breaking off suddenly in the middle of speaking, usually with the excuse of being overcome with emotion.
RC: **A66**

Notes: Aposiopesis is from the Greek word, ἀποσιώπησις, meaning to "become silent." This occurs when a speaker is overcome by a strong emotion (fear, joy, sorrow, etc...).

Apostrophe

Turning one's speech from one audience to another. Most often Apostrophe occurs when one addresses oneself to an abstraction, to an inanimate object, or to the absent.
RC: **A67**
Example: Angelo, in one line, speaks both to himself and a character in the scene:

"She speaks, and 'tis such sense that my sense breeds with it, --- Fare you well." – Shakespeare, *Measure for Measure, Act II Scene II*

Notes: Apostrophe, from the Greek word ἀποστροφή meaning to "to turn," is often seen as an exclamatory Rhetorical Figure of Speech. Apostrophe is often used to convey extreme emotion, as in Claudius's impassioned speech in Hamlet. It is the form of most asides in classical drama. It is a synonym of Prosphonesis and is related to other exclamatory devices such as Ecphonetic and Exclamation.

---

[4]   Edt. by Paul MacKendrick and Herbert M. Howe Madison. *Classics in translation, Volume I: Greek Literature.* 1966. Wisconsin: The University of Wisconsin Press.

Apothegm

One of several terms describing short, pithy sayings.

RC: **A68**

Example: "Don't count your chickens before they hatch." – Anonymous

Notes: Related terms/devices include Adage, Gnome, Maxim, Paroemia, Proverb, and Sententia.

Appositio

Addition of an explanatory or descriptive element.

RC: **A69**

Example: John Milton, **though blind**, saw the metaphysical realms far better than you or I could ever dream.

Ara

Cursing or expressing detest towards a person or thing for the evils they bring or for inherent evil.

RC: **A70**

Example: "Author of evil, unknown till thy revolt,
Unnam'd in Heav'n, now plenteous, as thou seest" – Michael in John Milton's *Paradise Lost*

Notes: Ara is a figure associated with the identification and detestation of evil. It is related to Deprecatio, Cataplexis, Ominatio, and Paraenesis.

Articulus

Placing phrases or words together without any conjunctions separating them.

RC: **A71**

Example: "We must... hold them, as we hold the rest of mankind, Enemies in War, in Peace Friends." – *US Declaration of Independence*

Notes: Articulus is closely related to both Braduse - concerned with pace – and Asyndeton – omitting conjunctions. It differs from Braduse, because it sets out a specific figure for accomplishing the effect of slower pace. Articulus can be seen as a figure beneath the broader term Braduse. It differs from Asyndeton, because Asyndeton deals with the omission of Conjunctions for any number of

Rhetorical effects, whereas Articulus is specifically a removal of conjunctions for the sake of pace.

Aschematiston

The use of plain, unadorned or unornamented language or the unskilled use of figurative language.
RC: **A72**

Notes: Often seen as the opposite of Macrologia. Although it is often thought of as a Vice, it has been considered to be the most effective means of Jest.

Asphalia

Offering oneself as a guarantee, usually in guarantee of another's reputation.
RC: **A73**

Notes: Asphalia is from the Greek word meaning "assurance."

Example: After slaying Caesar, Brutus attempts to appease the upset Romans, concluding with this instance of Asphalia: "With this I depart, that, as I slew my best lover for the good of Rome, I have the same dagger for myself, when it shall please my country to need my death." —Shakespeare, *Julius Caesar Act III Scene II*

Assonance

Repetition of similar vowel sounds, preceded and followed by different consonants, in the stressed syllables of adjacent words.
RC: **A74**
Example: "Or hear old Triton blow his wreathed horn. Or hear old Triton blow his wreathed horn." — William Wordsworth, *The World is Too Much with Us*

Notes: Assonance is a figure used mainly in poetry, and often considered a type of Alliteration. See Alliteration.

Assumptio

The introduction of a point to be considered, especially an extraneous argument.
RC: **A75**

Notes: Assumptio makes up a good portion of one's speech. It should be the task of the Rhetorician to replace this device (not completely), as well as others like it, with more effective figures in a more logical order.

Asteismus

Polite or gentle mockery. More specifically, figures of reply in which the answerer catches a certain word and re-launches it back to the first speaker with an unexpected twist.
RC: **A76**

Notes: Asteismus is best used in informal speeches, debate situations, and in informal writing. It should not be used as a figure of Oration and is related, loosely, to Paronomasia.

Astrothesia

A description of a star or stars.
RC: **A77**
Example: A trillion points of light filled the dark sky.

Notes: See Enargia.

Asyndeton

The omission of conjunctions between clauses, often resulting in a hurried rhythm or vehement effect.
RC: **A78**
Example: "We shall go on to the end, we shall fight in France, we shall fight on the seas and oceans, we shall fight with growing confidence and growing strength in the air, we shall defend our Island, whatever the cost may be, we shall fight on the beaches, we shall fight on the landing grounds, we shall fight in the fields and in the streets, we shall fight in the hills; we shall never surrender..." – Winston Churchill

Notes: Asyndeton, relative of Articulus and the opposite of Polysyndeton, is sometimes called Asyndetism. Its effective employment differs depending on whether it is being used in a speech or on paper. In writing its effectiveness lies in the opportunity to display many things as equally important. In speech its effectiveness is proportional to the use of pause and inflection. Asyndeton is related to Brachylogia (the absence of conjunctions between single words), and Polysyndeton (Excessive use of conjunctions).

Augendi Causa
Increasing volume or the use of inflection for emphasis.
RC: **A79**

Auxesis
Arranging words or clauses in a sequence of increasing force.
RC: **A80**
Example: Look, oh look, do you not see…see, oh see, this wound!

Avancer
Synonym of Auxesis.

Aversior
Latin synonym of Apostrophe.

B

Barbarism
The use of a word seemingly forced into a poem's meter; or the use of unconventional pronunciation.
RC: **B1**
Example: Do you commit to live and to lerve' To give and to serve? ("love'" is pronounced "lerve" to rhyme with "serve")

Notes: This device is often referred to as the "wretched rhyme" and is a very close relative of Antisthecon – identical in process; differing only in intent and Cacozelia. See Metaplasm.

Battologia
Vain repetition.
RC: **B2**

Bdelygmia
Expressing hatred and abhorrence of a person, word, or deed.
RC: **B3**
Example: "I do hate a proud man, as I do hate the engend'ring of toads." — Shakespeare, *Troilus and Cressida Act II scene III*

Notes: This can appear in many forms including abusive description of a character or his/her attributes, or by strong and inappropriate critique. This device is one which would stand consistent with an appeal to Pathos. If one has the desire to move his audience emotionally it is sometimes best to express like emotion toward a view or individual. Bdelygmia is a synonym of Abominatio.

Benedictio

A blessing, or the act of blessing.

RC: **B4**

Notes: Benedictio is a relative of Eullogia and is classically seen as a form of Antisigoge – a device meant for the beginning of the oration.

Bomphiologia

Exaggeration done in a self-aggrandizing manner, as a braggart.

RC: **B5**

Example: "I would to god my name were not so terrible to the enemy as it is. I were better to be eaten to death with a rust than to be scoured to nothing with perpetual motion." – Shakespeare, *Henry IV, Part 2 Act I Scene II*

Notes: See Macrologia.

Braduse

To slow the pace or delivery of one's speech – either to produce an emotional affect or to emphasize a certain point or idea.

RC: **B6**

Notes: Braduse can be used in two ways. First, one can use it to emphasize a point directly by slowing the speed of a certain line or phrase at the end of a particularly quick-paced section. Secondly, one can slow down a section prior to giving a main point. This lessens the amount of information being taken in by the audience before they receive the big idea. In order to make an effectively persuasive oration there must be colorful content as well as a *textured* delivery of that content – done by inflection, tone, and pace.

Brachylogia

The absence of conjunctions between single words.

RC: **B7**

Example: Love, hate, fear, joy, anger, pity, hope, guilt, disgust—the strongest emotions lead to the strongest conclusions.

Notes: Brachylogia is a relative of Asyndeton. Like Asyndeton, the result is a broken, hurried delivery. It can give equal importance to each term in a list or create a vehemence of expression. In a way, it is meant to overwhelm those who are listening or reading. It differs from Asyndeton in one aspect: Asyndeton is the absence of conjunctions between phrases and Brachylogia is the absence of conjunctions between single words.

Brevitas

A concise expression.

RC: **B8**

Notes: Brevitas is a compression of many facts or whole portions of speech into a subtler and usually much stronger version, and therefore works as a good partner to Metabasis or other such devices of summary and re-visitation.

C

Cacemphaton
An expression that is deliberately either foul or ill-sounding.
RC: **C1**
Example: Far too smelly. (Sounds like 'fart too smelly.')

Cacophonia
The joining of words that are harsh sounding.
RC: **C2**
Example: We would never stoop to your level, you grizzled band.

Notes: Often seen as a strong form of Excitatio.

Cacosistaton
An argument that is badly constructed – by form or content.
RC: **C3**

Notes: See Fallacy.

Cacosyntheton
When words are placed in the wrong order grammatically – done in a confused or awkward manner.
RC: **C4**
Example: The soup hot was in its bowl. (Instead of: the hot soup was in its bowl.)

Cacozelia

An attempt to show off using foreign or noble diction.

RC: **C5**

Example: Too long have lying lips loosed: *de hode perfecte incepere.*

Notes: Cacozelia is the negative use of Graecismus and Hebraism. See also Soraismus.

Catachresis

A harsh or fantastical Metaphor.

RC: **C6**

Example: The gas stove sparked like a solar flare. (Using such a gigantic thing as a solar flare as a Metaphor for such a small thing as a stove flare is implausible.)

Notes: See Metaphor.

Catacosmesis

Placing words or phrases in order of importance, prominence, or in time.

RC: **C7**

Example: I slept well; then I awoke, brushed my teeth, and went to school (time). Compare this poor bulb to the moon and greater still the sun (prominence).

Notes: "Catacosmesis, in Latine ordo, is a meete placing of words among themselves, wherof there be two kinds, the one when the worthiest word is set first, which order is naturall, as when we say: God and man, men and women, Sun and moone, life and death. And also, when that is first told that was first done, which is necessary and seemly. 'The other kind of order is artificiall, and in forme contrarie to this, as when the worthiest or weightiest word is set last: for the cause of amplifying, which the Rhetoricians cal Incrementum,: the description wherof shalbe set downe among the figures of Amplication.' 'The use of this first kind of order, doth most properly serve to the propertie and elegancy of speech, and due observation of nature and dignitie: which forme is well represented in the civil and solemne customs of nations, where the worthiest person are alwaies first named and highest plated.'" – Henry Peachum, *Garden of Eloquence*

Cataphasis

kind of Paralipsis in which one explicitly affirms the negative qualities that one has, and then passes over them.

RC: **C8**

Example: I refuse to say anything about this man's intense greed.

Notes: See Apophasis.

Cataplexis

Threatening or prophesying payback for ill doing.

RC: **C9**

Example: If you break the speed limit then you will get a ticket.

Notes: Cataplexis is a figure associated with consequence. It is related to Deprecatio, Ara, Ominatio, and Paraenesis.

Categoria

Exposing the evil or wickedness of one's adversary – usually in his presence.

RC: **C10**

Notes: A synonym of Accusatio.

Characterismus

The description of a persons' character.

RC: **C11**

Example: Beowulf has both a youthful heroism as a fearless warrior, and mature heroism as a reliable king.

Notes: Characterismus is a close relative of Ethopoeia. See Enargia.

Charientismus

Mocking someone playfully in order to settle their anger or frustration.

RC: **C12**

Example: Said to a fat man: I know your upset about losing all that money, but it will be ok, at least you are pregnant, right?

Notes: A type of Irony.

Chiasmus

Repetition of ideas in inverted order.

RC: **C13**

Notes: Chiasmus was particularly popular both in Greek and Latin literature, where it was used to articulate balance or order within a text. As a popular example, the Greek and Hebrew texts of the Bible also contain many long and complex Chiasmi (i.e. the Psalms). Recently, the term Chiasmus has come to mean any grammatical or thought structure that resembles a "Criss-Cross". In its classical application, however, Chiasmus would have been used for structures that do not repeat the same words and phrases (Like a Figure of Repetition), but instead it would create a mirrored effect upon the ideas and thoughts in a portion or passage. The elements of a simple Chiasmus are often labeled in the form A-B-B-A (The letters correspond to a inverse repetition of idea or grammatical structure). Although Chiasmus is considered a relative of Antimetabole, it is quite different in content composition.

Chleuasmos

A mocking answer which doesn't really answer an opponent's question.

RC: **C14**

Chorographia

The description of a particular nation.

RC: **C15**

Example: "FAR hence, amid an isle of wondrous beauty,

Crouching over a grave, an ancient, sorrowful mother,

Once a queen—now lean and tatter'd, seated on the ground,

Her old white hair drooping dishevel'd round her shoulders;

At her feet fallen an unused royal harp, Long silent—she too long silent—mourning her shrouded hope and heir; Of all the earth her heart most full of sorrow, because most full of love." – Walt Whitman, *Old Ireland*

Notes: See Enargia.

Chreia
Using an antidote which relates a saying or deed of something well known.
RC: **C16**
Example: And then he cut down the cherry tree.

Notes: See Adage.

Chronographia
Vivid representation of a certain historical or recurring time to create an allusion of reality.
RC: **C17**
Example: "Listen, my children and you shall hear
    of the midnight ride of Paul Revere.
    On the eighteenth of April in seventy-five,
    Hardly a man is now alive,
    that remembers that famous day and year." – Longfellow, *Paul Revere's Ride*

Notes: See Enargia.

Circumlocution
Talking around something by supplying a descriptive phrase to take its place.
RC: **C18**

Notes: This figure is often the means of the modern inside joke. Circumlocution can be a figure of avoidance, where the object is replaced so as not to say the actual thing, or it can be a figure of Irony, where the replacing phrase has a paradoxical or deeply descriptive relationship with the replaced phrase.

Climax
The point of greatest force – often the point of no return.
RC: **C19**

Notes: From the Greek word meaning "ladder."

Coenotes

Repetition of two different phrases: one at the beginning and the other at the end of successive paragraphs.

RC: **C20**

Example: "Give thanks to the LORD, for he is good, for his steadfast love endures forever. Give thanks to the God of gods, for his steadfast love endures forever. Give thanks to the Lord of lords, for his steadfast love endures forever." — Psalm 136:1-3 ESV

Notes: See Figures of Repetition.

Collocation

Two terms or words which, by use, are paired together in the mind of the hearer or speaker.

RC: **C21**

Example: Milk and Cookies, peanut butter and jelly, Bert and Ernie.

Notes: Collocation can be a type of Cliché or just a word grouping that, by cultures effect, has created an original tie between two words or thoughts.

Colon

A sort of *clause* – usually without a complete thought.

RC: **C22**

Example: You cannot expect me to believe this.

Commiseratio

Arousing emotion in the audience – more specifically pity.

RC: **C23**

Commoratio

Dwelling on or returning to one's strongest argument.

RC: **C24**

Comparatio

A comparison - a Metaphor, Simile, or Allegory.

RC: **C25**

Notes: Comparatio uses comparison to persuade by presenting one accepted or true concept as a relative of another not yet accepted concept (much like a Syllogism or Enthymeme of sorts) It is a device that relies heavily upon the knowledge of the audience. The success and effectiveness of Comparatio (or any other figure of Comparison) is fully dependent upon the understanding and common knowledge of the audience.

Common Guidelines:
1. A Comparatio must be made between two objects or ideas which both the audience and speaker know of or have experienced.
2. The Comparatio must be logical and not over exaggerated.
3. The Comparatio must evoke some emotional response.

Comprobatio
Approving and commending a virtue, especially in the hearers.
RC: **C26**
Example: Your kindness is endless. While I have been here, you have all treated me with love.

Notes: Comprobatio is often used as a strong beginning appeal. But in modern oratory, this device must be place after an Ethos is established and that only after a strong argument is raised.

Conceit
An extended Metaphor.
RC: **C27**

Notes: Popular during the Renaissance and typical of John Donne or John Milton. Unlike Allegory, which tends to have one-to-one correspondences, a Conceit typically takes one subject and explores the Metaphoric possibilities in the qualities associated with that subject. See Metaphor.

Concessio
Conceding a certain point or complete argument before it is stated or started.
RC: **C28**

Conclusio
The last part of an oration.
RC: **C29**

Notes: Conclusio is related to the following terms: Accumulatio, Proecthesis, Epiphonema, and Epetasis. It is the logical finish to any composition. Although simple to define, the Conclusion is the hardest part to control – as Longfellow said: "Great is the art of beginning, but greater is the art of ending."

Condescensio
The Latin synonym of Anthropopatheia.

Conduplicatio
The repetition of certain words, phrases, or clauses.
RC: **C30**
Example: Pray for the those that give up their lives. Pray for those that go before us. Pray for those that protect us.

Notes: Conduplicatio is a close relative of Traductio and a Figure of Repetition. See Figures of Repetition.

Congeries
Piling up words of differing meaning but for a similar emotional effect.
RC: **C31**
Example: Oh, fie, fie, fie! What **grief**, what **rage**, what **hopelessness**, what **madness**, oh, what **bitterness**!

Notes: Congeries is from the Latin, meaning a "heap."

Consonance
The repetition of consonants in words – usually stressed in the same place.
RC: **C32**
Example: "**W**hose **w**oods these are I think I know.
His **h**ouse is in the village though;
He will not **s**ee me **s**topping here

To watch his woods fill up with snow." – Robert Frost, *Stopping by Woods on a Snowy Evening*

Notes: A form of Alliteration. See Figures of Repetition.

Contentio
The Latin synonym for Antithesis.

Contrarium
Juxtaposing two opposite statements – usually to prove one as opposed to the other.
RC: **C33**
Example: The way to grandma's house is quite a pleasant walk, but the way to grandma's house is home to a wolf.

Notes: Contrarium is a relative of Syncrisis, Antitheton, Antithesis, Anthypophora, Apophasis, Enthymeme, and Prosapodosis.

Copia
Both a quality and quantity of excellent speech.

Correctio
The amending of a term or phrase just employed - redefinition.
RC: **C34**
Example: "These hedge-rows, **hardly hedge-rows, little lines of sportive wood run wild.**" – William Wadsworth, *Tintern Abbey*

Notes: Correctio is very closely related to Epanorthosis and other such Figures of Definition (Horismus). See Figures of Definition and Paraprosdokian.

D

Declamatio

Excessively ornamented and elevated speech about a hypothetical situation.
RC: **D1**

Declinatio

A digression.
RC: **D2**

Deesis

An expression of desire or need – usually made in conjunction with the name of a deity.
RC: **D3**
Example: "O God of battles, steel my soldiers' hearts! ...not today, o Lord. Oh, not today, think not upon the fault my father made in compassing the crown!" – Shakespeare, *Henry V Act IV Scene I*

Notes: Deesis is a close relative of Optatio.

Dehortatio

A statement meant to discourage.
RC: **D4**

Demonstratio

A vivid description. A synonym of Enargia.

Dendrographia
Vivid description of a tree in order to create a picture of reality.
RC: **D5**
Example: "The cherry trees bend over and are shedding,
On the old road where all that passed are dead,
Their petals, strewing the grass as for a wedding
This early May morn when there is none to wed." – Edward Thomas, *The Cherry Trees*

Notes: See Enargia.

Deliberative:
A type of Oration. See *Oration*.

Deprecatio
A prayer focused on the removal of some evil – weather in others or in oneself.
RC: **D6**
Example: "And going a little farther he fell on his face rand prayed, saying, 'My Father, if it be possible, let this cup pass from me; nevertheless, not as I will, but as you will.'" — Matthew 26:39 ESV

Notes: Deprecatio is related to Ara, Cataplexis, Ominatio, and Paraenesis.

Descriptio
An exposition of the consequences of an act.
RC: **D7**

Diacope
Repetition of a word with one or more words between them to express emotion.
RC: **D8**
Example: **All is finished**, forever...forever, **all is finished.**

Notes: Used to show great or deep emotion. See Figure of Repetition, Epizeuxis and Ploce.

Diaeresis
The logical division of a genus into its species or one syllable into two.
RC: **D9**
Example: Did you just say syl-l-la-ble?

Notes: See Metaplasm.

Dialogismus
Speaking as something or someone else.
RC: **D10**

Dialysis
To present alternatives – usually in detail.
RC: **D11**
Example: "If we are mark'd to die, we are enow, To do our country loss, and if to live,
The fewer men, the greater share of honor. God's will! I pray thee wish not one man more."
– Shakespeare, *Henry V Act IV Scene III*

Dianoea
The use of animated questions and answers to develop and argue a point.
RC: **D12**

Diaphora
The repetition of a common name.
RC: **D13**
Example: **Boys** will be **boys**.

Notes: See Figures of Repetition.

Diaskeue
Graphic description of circumstances intended to arouse the emotions.
RC: **D14**
Example: "Ay, but to die, and go we know not where;

To lie in cold obstruction and to rot;
This sensible warm motion to become
A kneaded clod; and the delighted spirit
To bathe in fiery floods, or to reside
In thrilling region of thick-ribbed ice;
To be imprison'd in the viewless winds,
And blown with restless violence round about…"- Shakespeare, *Measure for Measure act III scene I*

Notes: See Enargia.

Diastole
Taking a vowel sound or syllable and lengthening it out.
RC: **D15**
Example: **Oooooh** yeah!

Notes: See Metaplasm.

Diasyrmus
Using ridiculous comparison to reject an argument.
RC: **D16**

Diazeugma
An instance in which a subject governs several verbs or verb phrases.
RC: **D17**
Example: "He bites his lip and starts; Stops on a sudden, looks upon the ground, Then lays his finger on his temple; straight Springs out into fast gait, than stops again, strikes his breast hard…" - Shakespeare, *Henry VIII Act III Scene II*

Notes: See Zeugma.

Dicaeologia
When an individual admits to a charge against them but dismisses it out of necessity.
RC: **D18**

Example: "Prince: Father, you cannot disinherit me. If you be king, why should not I succeed? King Henry: Pardon me, Margaret, pardon me, sweet son, The Earl of Warwick and the Duke enforc'd me." —Shakespeare, *Henry VI Act 1 Scene 1*

Digressio
A departure from logical progression in an oration or informal speech.
RC: **D19**

Dilemma
Offering a choice between two alternatives to an opponent.
RC: **D20**
Example: Either you find your own way out, or I will help you.

Dirimens Copulatio
A statement which balances one thought with a contrary thought.
RC: **D21**

Distinctio
Producing clarity by explaining the definition of a term or phrase.
RC: **D22**

Notes: Distinctio is a Figure of Definition related to Horismus, Epanorthosis, Etc. See Figures of Definition.

Distributio
Divvying roles or duties up among a list of people.
RC: **D23**

Notes: Distributio is a kind of Divisio and a relative of Eutrepismus, Merismus, Synecdoche, Taxis, and Diaeresis.

Divisio
Dividing into classes or kinds.
RC: **D24**

Notes: Divisio is a relative of Distributio, Eutrepismus, Merismus, Synecdoche, Taxis, and Diaeresis.

E

Ecphonesis
An emotional exclamation.
RC: **E1**

Ecphrasis
A vivid description of an object.
RC: **E2**
Notes: Ecphrasis is usually a description of a commonplace object. See Enargia.

Ecthlipsis
The omission of either letters or syllables for the sake of poetic meter.
RC: **E3**
Example: Before time you waited thus
Built for the human's way
And in heaven's holy place all held
'Til peace's dying day.

Notes: A kind of Metaplasm. See Metaplasm.

Effictio
A vivid and usually verbal depiction of someone's body – in great detail.
RC: **E4**
Example: "My Lady's hair is threads of beaten gold;
Her front the purest crystal eye hath seen;
Her eyes the brightest stars the heavens hold;
Her cheeks, red roses, such as seld have been.
Her pretty lips, of red vermilion dye;
Her hand of ivory, the purest white…" – Bartholomew Griffin, *Fidesssa - Sonnet 39*

Notes: Effictio is a description of external appearance and deals with a head to toe evaluation. See Enargia.

Egressio
A Digression.

Elenchus
A logical refutation.

Notes: This type of argumentation is seen best in the dialogues of Socrates in which a question evokes a particular response.

Ellipsis
The omission of a word or phrase which is easily understood in the context.
RC: **E5**
Example: "And he to England shall along with you." – Shakespeare, *Hamlet Act III Scene iii* (The word "go" is understood in context)

Notes: See Zeugma.

Emphasis
To give special importance to a quality or trait.

Enallage
Adjusting a sentence so as to make it equivalent in thought but different grammatically.
RC: **E6**

Notes: Enallage is a "substitution of one case, person, gender, number, tense, mood, part of speech, for another. Word play of this sort was very common in inflected languages like Latin or Greek, which can make changes in case gender, number, etc. and still easily preserve the root word."[5]

---

[5]   See *Enallage* Richard Lanham's *A Handlist of Rhetorical Terms: Second Edition.* 1990. Los Angeles, University of California Press.

Enantiosis

Using opposite or contrary descriptions, usually in a paradoxical manner.

RC: **E7**

Example: If you do not master Rhetoric, you will become a slave to it.

Notes: See Irony.

Enargia

A vivid and lively description.

RC: **E8**

Notes: It is scientifically proven that the human mind can take in 110 bits of information at any one time. Listening to a human voice is on average, about 60 bits of information (the reason why most people cannot understand two voices simultaneously). In order to keep the audience from using the extra mind power to wander to other topics, the speaker must create deep thoughts in conjunction with images so that the listener has somewhere to go inside of the oration.

Kinds of Enargia:

1. **Anemographia:** A good and vivid description of wind – usually in an attempt to create a sense of reality.
2. **Astrothesia**: A description of a star or stars.
3. **Characterismus:** The description of a person's character.
4. **Chorographia:** The description of a particular nation.
5. **Chronographia**: Vivid representation of a certain historical or recurring time to create an allusion of reality.
6. **Dendrographia** - Vivid description of a tree in order to create a picture of reality.
7. **Ecphrasis:** A vivid description as to place an object before the mind's eye.
8. **Effectio**: A vivid and usually verbal depiction of someone's body – in great detail.
9. **Ethopoeia**: The description and portrayal of a character.
10. **Geographia:** Creating an illusion of reality by vividly describing the world.
11. **Hydrographia:** A vivid description of water in order to create a sense of reality.
12. **Hypotyposis:** A vivid description of a person, scene, action, condition, passion etc. used to create a sense of reality.
13. **Pragmatographia:** A vivid description of an action.

14. **Prosopographia:** The vivid description of someone's face or character...or a description of mystical or imaginary beings.
15. **Topographia:** A vivid description of a place.
16. **Topothesia:** A vivid description of an imaginary place.

Encomium
The praise of a person or thing.
RC: **E9**
Notes: Encomium praises by bringing up or emphasizing a trait or traits in an individual or thing.

Energia
A general term referring to the energy of an expression.
RC: **E10**
Notes: Energia is a relative of Excitatio.

Enigma
Obscuring one's meaning by presenting it in a way that purposely challenges the reader to understand.
RC: **E11**
Example: The poor are often found to be most rich.

Notes: Enigma is related to Skotison, Noema, Ennoia, and Schematismus.

Ennoia
Purposefully holding back information.
RC: **E12**

Notes: Ennoia is a relative of Skotison and Circumlocutio.

Enthymeme
A shortened Syllogism.
RC: **E13**

Notes: An Enthymeme is a Syllogism which uses premises that are only true generally. A Syllogism is a proof which has premises which are defiantly true.

Enumeratio
Division of a specific subject into its parts or points.
RC: **E14**
Example: "We formed in 1979, June, in Washington D.C. the Moral Majority, with a handful of people...which has grown now **to over a hundred thousand priests and rabbis and pastors and blacks and whites and young and old and all kinds. Catholics are the largest part of the constituency --** 30% -- because of our strong pro-life emphasis." —Jerry Falwell, The Role of Religion in Politics

Epagoge
A synonym for the inductive argument.

Epanalepsis
Repeating a phrase with a clause or phrase in between.
RC: **E15**
Example: "**I might**, unhappy word, O me, **I might**" - Sidney, *Astrophil and Stella, Sonnet 33*

Notes: See Figure of Repetition.

Epanodos
Repeating the main idea of an argument while presenting it in order to make it clearer.
RC: **E16**

Notes: Epanodos is a relative of Ploce and Polyptoton. See Figure of Repetition.

Epanorthosis
Altering or amending a thought to make it stronger or clearer.
RC: **E17**

Notes: Epanorthosis makes up a great deal of a composition. It is a relative of Correctio but differs in its content relationship with the statement prior. See Figures of Definition.

Epenthesis
The addition of a letter, sound, or syllable to the middle of a word.
RC: **E18**
Example: Many English-speaking people will add a 'p' to the word "warmth."

Notes: If the sound that is added is a consonant it is called Excrescence; if the sound that Is added is a vowel it is called Anaptyxis. See Metaplasm.

Epergesis
A clarifying apposition.
RC: **E19**
Example: Socrates did not consider himself to be a teacher, but instead he saw himself as a midwife, who, **having experience**, brought forth truth in others.

Notes: Epergesia is seen by most as a type of Epexegesis.

Epetasis
A concluding sentence intended to sum up and amplify what has just been said.
RC: **E20**
Example: That's it! You are grounded…**grounded forever!**

Epexegesis
When an interruption occurs in an oration or speech.
RC: **E21**

Epicrisis
Quoting a passage in order to comment either on it or to allow it to strengthen an argument or claim.
RC: **E22**

Notes: A relative of Exergasia.

Epideictic
A kind of Oration.

Epilogue
Using a previously stated statement or thought to infer what will come.
RC: **E23**
Example: "Did you perceive he did solicit you in free contempt when he did need your loves, and do you think that his contempt shall not be bruising to you when he hath power to crush."
– Shakespeare, *Coriolanus Act II Scene III*

Epilogus
Providing a foreshadowing of what is likely to come.
RC: **E24**

Epimone
A Figure of Repetition in which a plea is made over and over in the same words, or closely related words.
RC: **E25**
Example: "Who is here so base that would be a bondman? If any, speak; for him I have offended. Who is here so rude that would not be a Roman? If any speak; for him have I offended." - William Shakespeare, *Julius Caesar Act III Scene II*

Notes: A relative of both Exergasia and Epanorthosis. See Figures of Repetition.

Epistrophe
Ending a series of lines, phrases, clauses, or sentences with the same word or words.
RC: **E26**
Example: "When I was **a child**, I spoke as **a child**, and when I was **a child**, I played as **a child.**

Notes: Epistrophe is also known as Epiphora and Antistrophe. See Figure of Repetition.

Epiphonema
A summary in which the idea that was just presented is summed up in a pithy manner - an ornamental summary.
RC: **E27**

Epiplexis
Asking a question in order to chide or express grief.
RC: **E28**
Example: "Why died I not from the womb? why did I not give up the ghost when I came out of the belly?" — Job 3:11 ESV

Notes: See Figures of Questioning.

Episynaloephe
The act of blending two syllables into one.
RC: **E29**

Notes: See Metaplasm.

Epitheton
Ascribing to a person a certain attribute or characteristic.
RC: **E30**

Epitrochasmus
To touch rapidly on one point and then another.
RC: **E31**

Epitrope
Turning a point over to one's hearers in such a way as to prove something without stating it.
RC: **E32**

Epizeugma
Placing the verb that holds the entire sentence together either at the very beginning or the very ending of that sentence.

RC: **E33**

Example: Epizeugma at the beginning: Die they do when the plague comes.
Epizeugma at the end: Either by disease or age they die.

Epizeuxis

The repetition of words without any other words in between – mainly for emotional emphasis.

RC: **E34**

Example: Fie! Fie! Fie!

Notes: See Figures of Repetition.

Erotema

To ask a strong question as to affirm or deny something.

RC: **E35**

Example: Did you in fact kill him in cold blood?

Notes: See Figures of Questioning.

Erotesis

A question that does not need or imply a response.

RC: **E36**

Notes: See Figures of Questioning.

Ethopoeia

The description and portrayal of a character.

RC: **E37**

Example: "I felt very deeply his sorrow and his defeat. As things go in the animal kingdom, he is about my age, and when he lowered himself to creep under the bar, I could feel in my own bones his pain at bending so far." – E. B. White, *The Geese*

Notes: A very close relative of Characterismus and a kind of Enargia.

Ethos
An appeal for or to a person's character.
Notes: "Ethos names the persuasive appeal of one's character, especially how this character is established by means of the speech or discourse. Aristotle claimed that one needs to appear both knowledgeable about one's subject and benevolent. Cicero said that in classical oratory the initial portion of a speech (its exordium or introduction) was the place to establish one's credibility with the audience."[6]

The Three pillars of Ethos:
1. Practical skills & wisdom (*Phronesis*)
   - Experience
   - Leadership
   - Moderation
   - Discipline
   - Self-Control
2. Virtue, goodness (*Arete*).
3. Selflessness/personal sacrifices (*Eunoia*).

Eucharistia
To give thanks for something received.
RC: **E38**

Notes: Classically, Eucharistia is either audible or said in an aside.

Euche
A vow or promise.
RC: **E39**

Notes: Euche is closely related to Adhoratio, Orcos, and Eustathia.

Eulogia
Pronouncing a blessing for the goodness in a person.
RC: **E40**

Notes: See Encomium.

---

[6]   Gideon Burton's *Silva Rhetoricae* at humanities.byu.edu/rhetoric/Silva.htm.

Euphemism
Substitution of a more delicate term.
RC: **E41**
Example: Your father is in a better place.

Eustathia
Promising constancy in focus and feeling.
RC: **E42**

Notes: Eustathia is related to Adhortatio and Euche.

Eutrepismus
Numbering and pondering parts or points under consideration.
RC: **E43**

Notes: Eutrepismus is a figure of preparation. It numbers parts before an argument or points before a speech. Eutrepismus is a relative of Enumeratio, Distributio, and other figures of division.

Example
To expound upon a given point by presenting it, so it can be seen (or so it can be seen in a practical way).
RC: **E44**

Excitatio
To keep an audience from boredom by exciting them.
RC: **E45**

Notes: Excitatio is a form of Energia and is most commonly achieved through dramatic inflection, tone, and diction.

Excursus
A digression.
RC: **E46**

Exemplum

Using a mythical, magical, or illustrative story as a proof or example.

RC: **E47**

Notes: Aesop's fables could be considered a form of Exemplum.

Exergasia

Repetition of the same idea, changing either its wording or delivery.

RC: **E48**

Example:

"I take thy hand – this hand, As soft as dove's down and as white as it, Or Ethiopian's tooth, or the famn'd snow that's bolted by the northern blasts twice o'er." – Shakespeare, *The Winter's Tale, Act IV Scene IV*

Notes: Exergasia is often seen as a mixture of Epanorthosis and Correctio. See Figures of Repetition.

Exouthenismos

An expression of disgust.

RC: **E49**

Example: O inhabitant of Lebanon, nested among the cedars, how you will be pitied when pangs come upon you, pain as of a woman in labor!" — Jeremiah 22:23 ESV

Notes: A lesser form of Abominatio, Exouthenismos is a device which stands consistent with an appeal to Pathos. If one has the desire to move his audience emotionally it is sometimes best to express like emotion toward a view or individual.

Expeditio

After stating all the possibilities, the speaker eliminates all but one.

RC: **E50**

Example: You either came on a bus, a train, or an airplane. Since you are afraid of planes, and you always complain about the price of the train fare around here, you must have come on the bus.

Notes: Expeditio is a more specific form of Eutrepismus and a relative of Dialysis and Enumeratio.

Exuperatio
See Hyperbole.

Exuscitatio
Stirring up one's hearers by expressing personal feelings.
RC: **E51**

Notes: From the Greek word meaning to 'awaken' or 'arouse'. "...Genuine feeling in (one) begets a like feeling in (others) and convinces them of their sincerity."[7] This Device is the foundational connection between a plea of Pathos and Ethos. If one has the desire to move his audience emotionally, it is sometimes best to express like emotion toward a view or individual.

---

[7] See Miriam Joseph's *Shakespeare's Use of the Language Arts*. Paul Dry Books. 2005. The Trivium: The Liberal Arts of Logic, Grammar, and Rhetoric. 2002. Paul Dry Books, Inc.

F

Fallacy
A piece of an argument, or an argument as a whole, which provides poor or no support, by way of reasoning, to its conclusion.

List of major <u>content</u> related Fallacies:
Inappropriate Consequence: Drawing a conclusion from premises that do not support it.
Assuming A implies B on the basis that B implies A.
Example: If a person runs barefoot, then their feet hurt. Megan's feet hurt. Therefore, Megan ran barefoot.

Problem: Other things can result in foot pain.

Begging the Question: A conclusion which gathers its strength by means of premises that assume that conclusion.
Example: Person A: He is mad right now! Person B: How do you know? Person A: Well, because he is really angry.

Problem: The conclusion is already assumed from the premise.

Converse Fallacy of Accident: An argument made from a special case – which turns it into a general rule. Also called the Fallacy of Hasty Generalizations.
Example: Every time I see Josh he is painting; therefore, Josh is always painting.

Problem: What one sees of an individual is just a portion of that individual's life, therefore, they are unable to conclude that they do something all the time.

Denying the Antecedent: Drawing a conclusion from premises that do not support that conclusion. Not T implies Not Z on the basis that T implies Z.

Example: When I go to bed it is always dark outside, and right now it is light outside, therefore, I am not going to sleep.

Problem: The fact that it is daytime does not support the fact that one could not go to sleep.

Fallacy of Accident: Making a general statement that does not take into account special cases.
Example: Cutting people is a crime. Surgeons cut people. Therefore, surgeons are criminals.

Problem: Cutting people is only sometimes a crime.

Fallacy of Multiple Questions: Groups more than one question in the form of a single question.
Example: Do you still rob banks?

Problem: Whether a yes or no is given it still grants guilt upon the one asked. This is because two questions have been forced into one: Have you ever robbed a bank? And, "Do you rob banks now?

Fallacy of False Cause: Saying one thing is the cause of another without proof or a justifiable chain of happenings.
Example: I'm a smart kid, I'll never do drugs.

Problem: There is not necessarily a link between your brilliance and avoiding drug use. There are many factors which bring one into that situation.

Irrelevant Conclusion: Presets a conclusion which diverts attention away from the argument at hand – making the conclusion irrelevant.
Example: I like ice cream so much that everyone should have ice cream everyday to stay healthy.

Problem: The issue at hand might be the unhealthy habit of eating ice cream or just a question of what grants an individual health - either way, the conclusion that eating ice cream everyday just because one likes it is not a justifiable argument.

Straw Man: A fallacy which attacks a person's argument by presenting it poorly or completely wrong.

Example: Person 1: Days off are great. Person 2: They are, are they? Well, if every day was a day off then no one would ever work and we would all die of starvation and obesity. You are very wrong!

Problem: Person 2 has misrepresented what person 1 has said. He has taken a simple statement of delight and turned it into a fully-fledged argument in support of a conclusion it never meant to support.

List of major <u>verbal</u> related Fallacies:
Amphibology: A Fallacy founded in an unclear arrangement of thoughts – usually as a result of incorrect grammar.

Connotation Fallacies: When a debater quotes his opponent but does so by replacing his words with rude or inappropriate ones in an attempt to discredit.

Equivocation: Using an identical term throughout an argument, but changing the meaning depending on the circumstance.
Example: All heavy things have great mass, therefore, a thought which weighs heavily upon your mind is of great physical mass.

*Problem: The definition of **heavy** goes far beyond the explanation of great mass. For example, in the argument above, **heavy** refers to the importance of the thought.*

Division: An argument that takes an attribute of a whole and forces it upon its components or parts.
Example: Beantown high school is a really great school; therefore, each class is a great class and each student is a great student.

Problem: Just because the school as a whole is great does not mean that there are not some classes which are poorly constructed or that there are not some students who lack morality and/or ability.

Fallacy of Composition: An argument that takes an attribute of the pieces and forces it upon the whole.
Example: Every guy on the soccer team is an excellent player, therefore, the team is going to be great!

Problem: Although the team members might be skilled, it does not mean that the team will be great. For example: they may not be able to work well as a team.

Proof by Verbosity: A technique which attempts to overwhelm its opponents or those involved in the argument with a mass of information.

Figure of Definition
Rhetorical devices that define.
1. **Horismus** - A clear and concise definition.
2. **Epanorthosis** - Altering or amending a thought to make it stronger or clearer.
3. **Correctio** - The amending of a term or phrase just employed - redefinition.
4. **Parenthesis** - An explanatory or qualifying word, clause, or sentence.
5. **Synonymia** - The use of several synonyms in order to explain or amplify a given point.
6. **Restrictio** - Making an exception which restricts or limits what has been said.
7. **Epergesis** - A clarifying apposition.
8. **Distinctio** - Producing clarity by explaining the definition of a term or phrase.

Figure of Repetition:
Rhetorical devices that repeat a specific concept, phrase, group of words, a single word, or letter throughout a thought or sentence.
1. **Adnominatio:** Assigning to a proper name its literal or homophonic meaning.
2. **Alliteration:** Repetition of the same letter or sound within nearby words.
3. **Anadiplosis:** The repetition of the last word (or phrase) from the previous line, clause, or sentence at the beginning of the next. Often combined with climax.
4. **Anaphora:** Repetition of the same word or group of words at the beginning of neighboring clauses, sentences, or lines – granting emphasis to a particular phrase or word.
5. **Antaclasis:** The repetition of a word or phrase, but the meaning of the word changes the second time it is used.
6. **Antistasis:** The repetition of a word in a contrary sense.
7. **Assonance:** Repetition of similar vowel sounds, preceded and followed by different consonants, in the stressed syllables of adjacent words.

8. **Coenotes:** Repetition of two different phrases: one at the beginning and the other at the end of successive paragraphs.
9. **Conduplicatio:** The repetition of certain words, phrases, or clauses.
10. **Consonace:** The repetition of consonants in words – usually stressed in the same place.
11. **Commoratio:** Dwelling on or returning to one's strongest argument.
12. **Diacope:** Repetition of a word with one or more words between them to express emotion.
13. **Diaphora:** The repetition of a common name.
14. **Epanodos:** Altering or amending a thought to make it stronger or more clear.
15. **Epimone:** A figure of repetition in which a plea is made over and over in the same words, or closely related words.
16. **Exergasia:** Repetition of the same idea, changing either its wording or delivery.
17. **Epanalepsis:** Repeating a phrase with a clause or phrase in between.
18. **Epistrophe:** Ending a series of lines, phrases, clauses, or sentences with the same word or words.
19. **Epizeuxis:** The repetition of words without any other words in between – mainly for emotional emphasis.
20. **Homiologia:** Tedious and frivolous repetition.
21. **Isocolon:** A series of phrases or short clauses which are similarly structured and maintain the same length.
22. **Mesarchia:** The repetition of the same word or words at the beginning and middle of successive sentences.
23. **Mesodiplosis:** Repetition of the same word or words in the middle of successive sentences.
24. **Homoipototon:** Repetition of the same consonant in neighboring words.
25. **Paroemion:** Excessive Alliteration – almost every word in a sentence or thought is alliterated.
26. **Paromoiosis:** Parallelism of sound between the words of adjacent clauses whose lengths are equal or approximate to one another.
27. **Ploce:** The repetition of a word for emphasis.
28. **Polyptoton:** The repetition of a word by using a non-identical form.
29. **Polysyndeton:** Placing excessive conjunctions between clauses.
30. **Palilogia:** Repetition of the same word, with none between, for vehemence.

31. **Pleonasmus:** Use of redundant words, often to strengthen the thought - repetition that is grammatically unneeded.
32. **Symploce:** Beginning a series of lines, clauses, or sentences with the same word or phrase while simultaneously repeating a different word or phrase at the end of each element in this series.
33. **Synonymia:** The use of several synonyms in order to explain or amplify a given point.
34. **Tautologia:** The vane or wearisome repetition of the same idea in different words – wearisome Exergasia.
35. **Traductio:** Repeating the same word variously throughout a sentence or thought.

Figures of Questioning:

Rhetorical Figures which ask or use Questions.
1. **Anthypophora**: Reasoning done by asking oneself questions and then immediately answering them.
2. **Dianoea:** The use of animated questions and answers to develop an argument.
3. **Epipelxis**: Asking a question in order to chide or express grief.
4. **Erotema:** To affirm or deny a point strongly by asking it as a question.
5. **Erotesis:** A question that does not need or imply a response.
6. **Pysma**: The asking of multiple questions successively.
7. **Ratiocinatio:** Reasoning with oneself through questions.
8. **Subjectio**: Giving an answer to one's own question regarding how an argument should proceed.

Frequentatio

The bringing together of various points used throughout an argument and presenting them in a conclusion or summary in a more forceful and dramatic way.
RC: **F1**

Notes: Frequentatio is a relative of Climax.

G

Geographia

Creating an illusion of reality by vividly describing the world.

RC: **G1**

Example: The smell of damp earth, after the rain, surrounded the great stone mansion and folding it in wisps of fog while the early morning October sun peaked through the haze to adorn the brick wall with dappled simplicity.

Notes: See Enargia.

Gnome

One of several terms describing short pithy sayings.

RC: **G2**

Example: "A stitch in time saves nine." – Anonymous

Notes: See Adage.

Graecismus

Using Greek words, examples, or grammatical structures.

RC: **G3**

Example: There is only one word for love in the English language, which limits our communication of such a diverse affection. In Greek there are five different words for love – including *Agape,* which is the one we will focus on today.

Notes: Graecismus is a more specific form of Soraismus and a relative of Hebraism.

H

Hebraism:
Making use of a Hebrew content or form.
RC: **H1**

Notes: Hebraism is a more specific form of Soraismus and a relative of Graecismus.

Hendiadys
Using a conjunction to specifically create a complex and equal meaning between two words instead of subordinating one to the other.
RC: **H2**
Example: I have never been to Europe, but I hear it is *beautiful* **AND** *unforgettable*.

Hendiatris
When three words are used to capture or expose one main idea or concept.
RC: **H3**
Example: Wine, Women, and Song.

Notes: Hendiatris is related to Tricolon and Isocolon. Hendiatris is used most famously in modern times as the structure of the motto.

Heterogenium
Avoidance of a particular issue by changing the subject to something different.
RC: **H4**
Example: Person 1: Are you seeing anyone?
Person 2: So how 'bout the weather we've been having?

Notes: Heterogenium is a break from logic, which circumvents a particular subject, because there is no support or proper opposition for it.

Homiologia
Tedious and frivolous repetition.
RC: **H5**

Homoeoprophoron
Repetition of the same consonant in neighboring words.
RC: **H6**

Notes: Homoeoprophoron is much like the English term Consonance and is related to Alliteration. See Figures of Repetition.

Homoeosis
Using a comparison to energize or beautify your language and/or argument.
RC: **H7**

Notes: A relative of Comparatio and a general device including Metaphor, Homoeosis is a necessary element in any oration or presentation; it gives the audience something tangible for their senses to hold on to.

Homoioptoton
The repetition of the same case on the end of neighboring words.
RC: **H8**
Example: Oh, that your nat**ure** would undo your displeas**ure**.

Notes: See Figures of Repetition.

Homoioteleuton
Similarity of endings of adjacent or parallel words.
RC: **H9**
Example: That man is all together *eloquent*, powerfully *relevant*, and graciously *benevolent*.

Notes: See Figures of Repetition.

Horismus
A clear and concise definition.
RC: **H10**

Notes: See Figures of Definition.

Hydrographia
A vivid description of water in order to create a sense of reality.
RC: **H11**
Example:
"…Each laid on other a staying hand
To listen ere we dared to look,
And in the hush we joined to make
We heard, we knew we heard the brook.
A note as from a single place,
A slender tinkling fall that made
Now drops that floated on the pool
Like pearls, and now a silver blade." – Robert Frost, *Going for Water*

Notes: See Enargia.

Hymos
To make use of humor or comedy – the use of incongruity to cause laughter.
RC: **H12**
Example: There are two muffins sitting in an oven, the first one turns to the other and says, "Wow! It's really getting hot in here." The other muffin, in surprise, responds, "Ahhhh! A talking muffin!"

Notes: This figure relies upon Irony and Anesis (or other related figures) to invoke within the audience a response of amusement or laughter.

Hypallage
Reversing the order of words – usually reversing also the relationship between two concepts, objects, or ideas.

RC: **H13**
Example: The luster's diamond, replaces: the diamond's luster.

Notes: Hypallage is a device of emphasis. It should only be used to emphasize an attribute over its object (like in the example above) or one idea over another. It gives the audience a taste of what is important to you or to the argument.

Hypocrisis
Mimicking someone's speech or gestures in a mocking way.
RC: **H14**

Notes: Hypocrisis is a mixture of Sarcasmus and Sermocinatio/Dialogismus.

Hyperbaton
An inversion of regular word order.
RC: **H15**
Example: Oh, to be a **flower blooming**, And **upward toward the sun peek**.

Hyperbole
Excess or exaggeration.
RC: **H16**
Example: I'm so hungry I could **eat a horse**.

Notes: Hyperbole is used to create emphasis. It is a literary device often used in poetry, and it is frequently encountered in more casual environments as a source of Irony or comedy. It is also a visual technique in which a deliberate exaggeration of a particular part of an image is employed.

Hypotyposis
A vivid description of a person, scene, action, condition, or passion.
RC: **H17**
Example:
"Ere-while of Musick, and Ethereal mirth,
Wherwith the stage of Ayr and Earth did ring,
And joyous news of heav'nly Infants birth,
My muse with Angels did divide to sing;

But headlong joy is ever on the wing,
In Wintry solstice like the shortn'd light
Soon swallow'd up in dark and long out-living night." – John Milton, *Passion*

Notes: This device is used to create a sense of reality. See Enargia.

Hypozeugma

A construction of phrases or words of equal strength or importance being placed before the word on which they all rely.
RC: **H18**
Example: "Meanwhile, impatient to mount and ride, Booted and spurred, with a heavy stride on the opposite shore walked Paul Revere." - Henry Wadsworth Longfellow, *Paul Revere's Ride*

Notes: Hypozeugma is a figure of emphasis.

Hypozeuxis

Every clause has its own verb.
RC: **H19**
Example: "The women **sat,** the men **stood**, and the children **ran** amuck. The festival had begun and the game was a foot."

Hysterologia

A Hyperbaton in which one interposes a phrase between a preposition and its object.
RC: **H20**
Example: The man followed me **like a hungry lion follows his prey** to capture me in some way or another.

Hysteron Proteron

Disorder of Time – where what should be first, second, third, etc. is not in logical order.
RC: **H21**
Example: Bake the cake and purchase the ingredients for it.

I

Icon
Painting the likeness of a person by imagery.
RC: **I1**
Example: Said of Helen of Troy: "Was this the face that launch'd a thousand ships And burnt the topless towers of Ilium?" – Christopher Marlowe, *Dr. Faustus*

Inopinatum
The expression of one's inability to believe or conceive of something.
RC: **I2**

Notes: A relative of Adynata.

Insinuatio
A method for securing good will within the introductory section of a discourse.

Interrogatio
Making use of a question to strengthen an argument.
RC: **I3**
Example: "While, therefore, you were doing and saying and negotiating all of these things, were you not alienating the republic's allies?" — *Ad Herennium*

Notes: See Figures of Questioning.

Inter se Pugnantia
Using direct address to reprove someone before an audience – done usually by making clear the contradictions between someone's actions and deeds.
RC: **I4**

Intimation

Hinting at a meaning but not stating it explicitly.

RC: **I5**

Notes: Intimation is a relative of Paralipsis, Significatio, and Occultatio.

Irony

Speaking in such a way as to imply the contrary of what one says, often to accomplish ridicule, mockery, or jest.

RC: **I5**

Isocolon

A series of phrases or short clauses which are similarly structured and maintain the same length.

RC: **I6**

Example: Protect our homes, protect or village, protect our nation - protect our freedom!

Notes: Isocolon is a relative of Tricolon and Hendiatris.

K

Kairos

Refers to the best or most appropriate time to give a particular speech.

Notes: The term Kairos generally refers to the way a given context for communication both calls for and constrains one's speech. Thus, sensitive to Kairos, a speaker or writer takes into account the contingencies of a given place and time; and considers the opportunities within this specific context for words to be effective and appropriate to that moment. As such, this concept is tightly linked to considerations of audience (the most significant variable in a communicative context) and to decorum (the principle of apt speech). Rhetorical analysis of any sort begins with some orientation to the Kairos. Whether or not a Rhetorical critic employs the term Kairos, he or she will examine the contingencies and constraints of place, time, culture, and audience that affect choices made by speakers and authors to influence that moment. Germany, of post-World War I, was demoralized and disorganized. Adolph Hitler's Rhetoric was successful not only because of his personal charisma and his mastery of delivery, but because he spoke at the right time. The German people wanted a way out of its economic morass and its cultural shame, and Hitler provided them both with his strong, nationalistic oratory. Had Germany been doing better economically, Hitler's words would have bounced harmlessly off the air.[8]

---

[8]   See Gideon Burton's *Silva Rhetoricae on* humanities.byu.edu/rhetoric/Silva.htm. 1996. Viewed on Oct. 9, 2009.

L

Litotes

Deliberate understatement – usually when one expresses a thought by denying its opposite.

RC: **LI**

Example: He is not unfamiliar with the poems of Poe. (Meaning: He is quite familiar with the Poems of Poe.)

Notes: Litotes is an Ironic way to present material.

Logos

An appeal to reason or to the mind.

Notes: Aristotle, in his book on Rhetoric, voiced the desire that all communication be drenched with this appeal. At the same time, he realized that, because the mind of man is weak, we would need the other two appeals. This appeal is the most necessary of the three, since it holds the actual material of an argument.

Pillars of Logos:
1. Inductive and Deductive reasoning
   a. Example
   b. Enthymeme
2. Evidence
3. Facts
4. Proofs
5. Syllogism
6. "If...then" statements

M

Macrologia
Using more words than necessary to appear eloquent.
RC: **M1**

Notes: Macrologia refers to someone who is not only long-winded, but long-winded in a conversational way. Macrologia is the opposite of Copia.

Malapropism
An error or fallacy created by an attempt at eloquence – usually vulgar.
RC: **M2**

Notes: Malapropism is a form of Cacozelia and is related to Macrologia.

Martyria
Confirming something by referring to personal experience.
RC: **M3**
Example: "Before my God, I might not this believe without the sensible and true avouch of mine own eyes." – Shakespeare, *Hamlet Act I Scene I*

Notes: Martyria should be used if the speaker's character (Ethos) has already been established. If the audience does not know the speaker then this device should be replaced by Apodixis.

Maxim
Short pithy statement – usually a call to action or a concise statement of wisdom.
RC: **M4**
Example: Don't drown the man who taught you to swim.

Notes: See Adage and Protrope.

Medela
Consoling a friend or the actions of a friend when they do something indefensible.
RC: **M5**

Meiosis
A type of exaggeration which diminishes an object's or idea's nature.
RC: **M6**

Membrum
Roughly equivalent to a clause in English but with emphasis on completion of the first clause.

Notes: Membrum is a clause that is associated with the completion of a thought. In order to identify it, one must determine whether or not the clause's presence completes a previously started thought.

Mempsis
Expressing a complaint and seeking help.
RC: **M7**
Example: "How long, O Lord? Will you forget me forever? How long will you hide your face from me? How long must I take counsel in my soul and have sorrow in my heart all the day? How long shall my enemy be exalted over me? Consider and answer me, O Lord my God; light up my eyes, lest I sleep the sleep of death" – Psalms 13:1-3 ESV

Notes: Mempsis is a type of Protrope.

Merismus
Dividing of a whole into its parts.
RC: **M8**

Notes: A relative of Eutrepismus.

Mesarchia
Repeating identical words at the end and in the middle of neighboring clauses.
RC: **M9**

Example: "They **shall dwell** in the land that I gave to my servant Jacob, where your fathers lived. They and their children and their children's children **shall dwell** there forever, and David my servant shall be their prince forever." — Ezekiel 37:25 ESV

Notes: Mesarchia is a type of Metaplasm and a Figure of Repetition. See Metaplasm and Figures of Repetition.

Mesodiplosis
Repeating an identical word or a set of words in the middle of neighboring clauses.
RC: **M10**
Example: "We are afflicted in every way, **but not** crushed; perplexed, **but not** driven to despair; 9 persecuted, **but not** forsaken; struck down, **but not** destroyed." – 2 Corinthians 4:8-9 ESV

Notes: See Figure of Repetition.

Mesozeugma
A Zeugma in which one places a common verb for many subjects in the middle of a construction.
RC: **M11**
Example: First the water began to **run**, and then he did as well.

Notes: See Zeugma.

Metabasis
A transitional statement in which one explains what has been and what will be said.
RC: **M12**
Example: The matters you have heard were wonderful, and those that you shall hear are no less marvelous.

Notes: Metabasis is considered a Figure of Repetition and an Antisigoge.

Metalepsis

Referring to something by using a name or names that are only remotely related to it.
RC: **M13**
Example: Starches, proteins, and carbohydrates have become the center of our holidays. ("starches," "proteins," and carbohydrates" are used to talk of holiday meals)

Metallage

When a word or phrase is treated as the object inside another expression.
RC: **M14**
Example: "A lady's 'verily' is as potent as a lord's." — Shakespeare, *The Winter's Tale Act I Scene I*

Metaphor

A comparison made by referring to one thing as another.
RC: **M15**
Example: "**Life's** but a walking **shadow**; a poor **player,** that struts and frets his hour upon the stage." - Shakespeare, *Macbeth*

Notes: Metaphor was popular during the Renaissance and typical of John Donne or John Milton. When a Metaphor is extended, it becomes either a Conceit or an Allegory. See Conceit and Allegory.

Metaplasm

To mold a word differently – usually done for meter or eloquence.
RC: **M16**
Example: **Oft'** have I looked upon these woods.

Notes: **Kinds of Metaplasm which add to the word**:
1. **Diastole** - Taking a vowel sound or syllable and lengthening it out. (Example: oooooh yeah!)
2. **Epenthesis** – The addition of a letter, sound, or syllable to the middle of a word. (Example: The word "warmth" is said with the stop consonant: "P.")
3. **Paragoge** – The addition of a letter or syllable to the end of a word. (Example: "sore" becomes "sorel.")

4. **Prothesis** - The addition of a letter or syllable to the beginning of a word. (Example: "walking" becomes "awalking.")
5. **Diaeresis** – The logical division of a genus into its species or one syllable into two. (Example: "co-operate" becomes "cooperate.")

Kinds of Metaplasm which subtract from the word:
1. **Aphaeresis** – The omission of a syllable or letter at the beginning of a word. (Example: "until" becomes "till.")
2. **Apocope** – Omitting a letter or syllable at the end of a word.
3. (Example: "photography" becomes "photo.")
4. **Ellipsis** - The omission of a word or phrase which is easily understood in the context.
5. **Ecthlipsis** - The omission of either letters or syllables for the sake of poetic meter. (Example: "until" becomes "'till.")
6. **Synaeresis** - When two syllables are contracted into one. (Example: When New Orleans is pronounced "Nawlens.")
7. **Syncope** - Cutting letters or syllables from the middle of a word. (Example: "Library" becomes "Library.")
8. **Systole** - The act of making short a long vowel sound.

A kind of Metaplasm which works by transposition:
1. **Metathesis** – The switching of two or more letters in a word. (Example: "center" becomes "centre.")

Kinds of Metaplasm which work by substitution:
1. **Antisthecon** – The substitution in the middle of a word. (Example: "Reward" becomes "reword.")
2. **Barbarism** – The substitution at the end of a word. (Example: "Love" becomes "Lerve.")

Metastasis
The act of denying and turning an argument, made against you, against your adversary.
RC: **M17**
Example: "When Ahab saw Elijah, Ahab said to him, 'Is it you, you troubler of Israel?' 18 And he answered, 'I have not troubled Israel, but you have, and your father's house, because you have abandoned the commandments of the LORD and followed the Baals.'" —1 Kings 18:17-18 ESV

Metathesis

The transposition of letters within a word.

RC: **M18**

Example: "Theatre" becomes "theater."

Notes: Metathesis is a type of Metaplasm.

Metonymy

Reference to something or someone by naming one of its attributes.

RC: **M19**

Example: The redhead is coming.

Notes: Metonymy is a relative of Metalepsis.

Mimesis

The imitation of another's gestures, pronunciation, or utterance.

RC: **M20**

Example: The enemy said, "I will pursue, I will overtake, I will divide the spoil; my lust shall be satisfied upon them; I will draw my sword, my hand shall destroy them." —Exodus 15:9 [2]

Notes: Mimesis is related to Sermocinatio, Dialogismus, Ethopoeia, and Prosopopoeia.

Mycterismus

A mock given with an accompanying gesture.

RC: **M21**

N

Noema
An obscure and subtle speech.
RC: **N1**

Notes: A relative of Skotison – same in form but, perhaps, different in purpose.
It is also loosely related to Allegory, Enigma, and Schematismus.

O

Obsecratio
See Deesis.

Obtestatio
See Deesis.

Obticentia
See Aposiopesis.

Occultatio
Stating something while pretending to pass it by.
RC: **O1**
Example: I will not get into all the research I have done concerning this topic, but…

Notes: Occultatio is a relative of Intimation, Significatio, and Paralipsis.

Ominatio
A prophesy telling of evil to come.
RC: **O2**
Example: On the coming of the Anti-Christ: "Who is the liar but he who denies that Jesus is the Christ? This is the antichrist, he who denies the Father and the Son." - 1 John 2:22 ESV

Notes: Ominatio is a figure associated with the identification and detestation of evil. It is related to Deprecatio, Cataplexis, Ara, and Paraenesis. See Cataplexis and Paranesis.

Onedismus
Reprimanding someone for being wicked or ungrateful.
RC: **O3**

Onomatopoeia
Using or inventing a word whose sound imitates that which it names.
RC: **O4**
Example: Roar!

Optatio
Expressing a desire.
RC: **O5**
Example: Bring me my smoking jacket!

Notes: The strongest use of Optatio is in conjunction with promises or threats/warnings. It makes a fuller appeal and a much stronger ally if certain things are said to come true if your desire is met or, on the opposite side, if your desire is not fulfilled then something terrible will occur.

Oratory
Oratory refers to the ancient art of formal speech making. From the time of the ancient Geeks, Oratory has been studied as subordinate to Rhetoric. See Rhetoric.

Orcos
Swearing that a statement is true.
RC: **O6**
Example: Upon my mother's grave, I swear it is so.

Notes: Orcos is related to Euche, Adhoratio, and Eustathia.

Oxymoron
A compressed and apparent paradox.
RC: **O7**
Example: "I must be cruel only to be kind." – Shakespeare, *Hamlet*

Notes: Oxymoron is a relative of Paradox, Irony, and Synoeciosis.

P

Padeuteria

"A poem giving thanks to teachers for what we have been taught, or to God for our teachers."[9]

RC: **P1**

Example: It is truly not the pillars, nor the walls which hold this school up, nor is it the foundation physical on which we have built or education. It is the teachers, the teachers are the pillars of our learning, the walls of our education, and the foundations of our thought. And we praise God, the Great Teacher, who has taught them to teach.

Notes: Padeuteria is often looked on as more of a genre than a device in Rhetoric and is all but extinct in formal oratory.

Paenismus

An Expression of joy resultant of an obtained blessing or an avoided evil.

RC: **P2**

Example: "O, she's warm! If this be magic, let it be an art Lawful as eating." – Shakespeare, *The winter's Tale Act V Scene III* (This is an expression of joy when King Leontes discovers his wife is not dead like he imagined for 16 years)

Notes: Paenismus is a relative of Ecphonesis and Exclamatio.

Palilogia

Repetition of the same word, with none between, for vehemence.

RC: **P3**

Example: Oh, how useless is the blood of bulls, **lost, lost, lost**! All lost.

---

[9]   Sonnino, Lee A. A Handbook to Sixteenth-Century Rhetoric. 1968. London: Routedge and Kegan Paul.

Notes: Palilogia should be used sparingly – in climax or for emphasis. It is one of the strongest Figures of Repetition. Its closest relatives are Anadiplosis and Iteratio.

Palindrome

A word, sentence, phrase, or poem which reads the same forward and backward.
RC: **P4**
Example: Was it a rat I saw? (Palindrome of letters)
Fall leaves after leaves fall. (Palindrome of whole words)

Notes: Palindromes, by their very nature, are not suited to formal Oratory, but can be quite appealing in written forms. Palindrome is usually considered to be a compressed and strong form of Chiasmus.

Parable

The explicit drawing of a parallel between two essentially dissimilar things, especially with a moral or didactic purpose.
RC: **P5**

Notes: The Parable found its most popular form in the New Testament. Christ comments that his use of them is to obscure the Truth (Skotison) as much as to make it known. Parables can be powerful teachers, but if not properly used, or if the audience is not taken into consideration, then the lesson, like the truth in the parable above, will fall on deaf ears. The Parable is a close relative of Allegory, Conceit, and Simile – except its express purpose is to teach.

Paradiastole

To praise someone or something inappropriately or to bring out good qualities or virtues in a person when they are not present.
RC: **P6**
Example: (Said of a thief) He is just a good magician – who never gives anything back.

Notes: Paradiastole usually is a praise that is made up of contrasting concepts. The original meaning is: "a putting together of dissimilar things" and this may be in terms of either ideas or diction.

Paradiegesis
An introduction to a speech – usually told in narrative style.
RC: **P7**

Paradigma
A dissuading argument – usually making use of an Example or Comparatio.
RC: **P8**

Paradox
A statement opposed to common sense, but indeed contains some truth.
RC: **P9**
Example: "What a pity that youth must be wasted on the young." – George Bernard Shaw

Notes: Paradox is a strong and sometimes pithier relative of Oxymoron, Erotema, Aphora, and Irony.

Paraenesis
A warning of impending evil.
RC: **P10**
Notes: Paraenesis, classically, deals with moral or religious topics. It is a device of advice as much as of warning. It is a figure associated with the identification and detestation of evil. It is related to Deprecatio, Cataplexis, Ominatio, and Ara.

Paragoge
The addition of a letter or syllable to the end of a word.
RC: **P11**
Example: "If sore be sore, then L to sore makes fifty sores o' sorel" —Shakespeare, *Love's Labour's Lost 4.2.59-61*

Notes: See Metaplasm.

Paralipsis
Drawing attention to something, often by simply stating it, while pretending to ignore it.

RC: **P12**
Example: (In the following example, the idea that something is wrong or unscrupulous about this particular guy is presented without stating anything in its support. Not even the fact that something is wrong with him is stated.) "I don't have to tell you not to avoid that guy. Right?"

Notes: Paralipsis is a kind of Irony and a relative of Intimation, Significatio, and Occultatio. See Apophasis.

Parallelism:
Creating a similar structure in a specific couplet or series of related words, phrases, or clauses.
RC: **P13**
Example: Tomas Mitch is correct and Dan Allen is wrong.

Notes: Parallelism is best achieved by making use of other figures – such as: Antithesis, Anaphora, Asyndeton, Symploce, etc.

Paramythia
An expression aimed to console or comfort.

Example: "Be not afraid of greatness: some are born great, some achieve greatness, and some have greatness thrust upon 'em." – Shakespeare, *Twelfth Night Act II Scene V*

Paranthesis
Insertion of a qualifying word, clause, or sentence.
RC: **P14**
Example: "If I had married him, **after all he was in women's apparel**; I would not have had him."
– Shakespeare, *Marry Wives of Windsor Act V Scene v*

Notes: Paranthesis is a broad category containing Epanorthosis, Exergasia, and Correctio. See Figures of Definition.

Paracbasis
Turning aside from the main subject of the argument or speech.
RC: **P15**

Notes: Paracbasis is a form of digression.

Paraprosdokian
An unexpected ending to a phrase, clause, or sentence.
RC: **P16**
Example: I would be an excellent president, If I wasn't a blue jay.

Notes: Paraprosdokian is a form of Correctio, but goes beyond the normal nature of that particular figure. It incorporates Paradox, Irony, or some other related device to give an unexpected or surprising twist o the end. Because of this, it is used like Paradoxical figures, for emphasis by way of humorous or dramatic effect. See Anesis and Hymos.

Paregmenon
A general term for the repetition of a word or a word that is related.
RC: **P17**
Example: "O villain, villain, smiling, damned villain!" – Shakespeare, *Hamlet Act I Scene v*

Notes: See Figures of Repetition.

Parelcon
The use of redundant or unnecessary terms - often the use of two words where one is sufficient.
RC: **P18**

Parembole
An interruption – often seen as purposeful.
RC: **P19**

Notes: Closely related to Parenthesis. Parembole is an interruption that is more closely related to the main subject or argument then Parenthesis.

Pareuresis
To make a genuine excuse.
RC: **P20**
Example: I apologize for being late; my son was in the hospital.

Paroemia
A short, pithy saying.
RC: **P21**
Example: "The only thing we have to fear is fear itself." – Franklin D. Roosevelt

Notes: See Adage.

Paroemion
Excessive Alliteration.
RC: **P22**
Example: **P**eter **P**icked a **P**lace that would **P**rovide the **P**erfect view.

Notes: See Alliteration.

Paromoiosis
He similarity of sound between the words of adjacent clauses whose lengths are either equal or approximate to one another.
RC: **P23**
Example: "Do not let us speak of darker days; let us speak rather of sterner days. These are not dark days: these are great days." – Winston Churchill, *To the Boys of Harrow School*

Notes: see Homeoteleuton.

Paromologia
Admitting to a particular fault in order to create a favorable conclusion.
RC: **P24**
Example: Yes, you're right…I did hate her, **but** I didn't kill her.

Paronomasia

Using words that sound alike but differ in meaning.

RC: **P25**

Example: "The dying Mercutio: Ask for me tomorrow and you shall find me a grave man." – Shakespeare, *Romeo and Juliet*

Notes: Paronomasia is a relative of Antanaclasis, however it differs slightly because Antanaclasis creates puns by using identical words with different meanings, whereas Paronomasia can pun by using words that merely sound similar or have a relation to a certain word (like in the above example).

Parrhesia

Speaking bluntly or the act of asking forgiveness for speaking bluntly.

RC: **P26**

Pathopoeia

An appeal to the hearers' emotions and an attempt to arouse them by showing one's own feelings.

RC: **P27**

Notes: Pathopoeia is related to Deesis, Ecphonesis, and Indignatio.

Pathos

An appeal to the emotions.

Notes: Pathos is an appeal designed to evoke and engage the emotions and more pragmatically it "...is that form of persuasion by which one endeavors to put the auditor into whatever frame of mind is favorable to one's purpose."[10] This **frame of mind** is crucial to the process of persuasion, how one feels will directly affect how he will conclude and how he will act. "... When people... feel friendly to the man who comes before them for judgment, they regard him as having done little wrong, if any; when they feel hostile, they take the opposite

---

[10]   Joseph, Miriam. *The Trivium: The Liberal Arts of Logic, Grammar, and Rhetoric.* 2002. Paul Dry Books, Inc.

view. ""[11] Cicero encouraged the use of Pathos at the conclusion of an oration, but emotional appeals are, of course, more widely viable. Aristotle's Rhetoric contains a great deal of discussion of affecting the emotions; categorizing the kinds of responses of different demographic groups. Thus, we see the close relations between assessment of Pathos and of audience. Pathos is also the category by which we can understand the psychological aspects of Rhetoric. Criticism of Rhetoric tends to focus on the overemphasis of Pathos (emotion) at the expense of Logos (the message).

Two Guidelines for Pathos:
1. Pathos is best adorned with simple language.
2. Pathos, in order to be lastingly effective, must be under control.

Periergia
The overuse of a word or figures of speech.
RC: **P28**
Example: **Peter P**icked a **P**lace on the **P**laques which would **P**rovide the most **P**revalent standing.

Notes: Periergia is a form of Macrologia.

Period
Suspending the primary thought of a sentence until its conclusion.
RC: **P29**
Example: The sentence's main verb "sing" is placed at the end of a long thought:

"Of man's first disobedience and the fruit
Of that forbidden tree, whose mortal taste
Brought death into the world, and all our woe,
With loss of Eden, till one greater Man
Restore us, and regain the blissful seat,
Sing Heav'nly Muse..." – John Milton, *Paradise Lost*

Notes: Period has evolved into the definition stated above, but classically (and still in spirit) the Period was just a unit of measurement – a Period was one

---

[11] Aristotle, The Art of Rhetoric. 1982. Trans. John Henry Freese. Loeb Classical Library.

complete thought, from beginning to end. In Aristotle's Rhetoric it is defined like this: "By a period I mean a portion of speech that has in itself a beginning and an end, being at the same time not too big to be taken in at first glance...A period may either be divided into several members or remains simple."[12]

Periphrasis
When a descriptive word takes the place of a proper noun or name.
RC: **P30**
Example: The day of Christmas is a **day of joy**.

Notes: Periphrasis is a relative of Circumlocution.

Perissologia
Wordiness.
RC: **P31**

Notes: A relative of Periergia and a type of Macrologia. See Macrologia.

Peristasis
A description of circumstances which support the main point or thought (who, when, where, and why).
RC: **P32**
Example: I know now that it was Mr. Dale Everate who killed the mayor. He did it in the back of that old barn were the pigs used to sleep, all huddled for warmth, and he did it with my gun...it was not I who pulled the trigger, but he!

Notes: See Enargia.

Perversio
See Anastrophe.

Personification
Talking of inanimate objects as though they had human qualities or abilities.
RC: **P33**

---
[12]   Ibid.

Example: The stars winked at me. (The verb 'winked' is an action which humans do and therefore it is a Personification for an inanimate object like a star to do so)

Philophronesis
Using mild and soft speech to calm an adversary.
RC: **P34**

Petitio Principii
A Fallacy which occurs when the premise of an argument says the same thing as the conclusion, but in different words – more a kind of repetition (Epanorthosis) than gaining logical ground.
RC: **P35**
Example: Peace is accompanied by solitude and solitude by peace, and, therefore, solitude is synonymous with peace.

Pleonasm
Use of redundant words, often to strengthen the thought - repetition that is grammatically unneeded.
RC: **P36**
Example: I do not want anyone to be there, not the wise or the rich or the powerful. (Wise, rich, and powerful are unneeded because it was already stated that no one was to come)

Ploce
The repetition of a word for emphasis.
RC: **P37**
Example: "Make war upon themselves - brother to brother / Blood to blood, self against self."
– Shakespeare, *Richard III*

Notes: Ploce is a Figure of Repetition. See Figures of Repetition.

Polyptoton
The repetition of a word by using a non-identical form.
RC: **P38**
Example: "With eager **feeding food** doth choke the **feeder**." — Shakespeare, *Richard II Act II Scene I*

Notes: See Figures of Repetition.

Polysydeton
Placing excessive conjunctions between clauses.
RC: **P39**
Example: I walked through the woods **and** I didn't see the light **and** I didn't see any sunshine. I didn't hear a sound **and** I didn't know where I was **and** I didn't really care **and** I didn't really care about not caring.

Notes: Used to slow or create a particular rhythm or to emphasize many points as having the same quality. Polysydeton is a crucial supporter of Braduse.

Pragmatographia
The description of an action.
RC: **P40**
Example: He stabbed with all his might and with all the weight of his body behind the thrust.

Notes: Classically, Pragmatographia is frequently used in drama for exposition or to report what happened offstage. See Enargia.

Praeteritio
A pretended omission.
RC: **P41**

Notes: Synonym of Paralipsis.

Procatalepsis
Refutation of oncoming objections to an argument.
RC: **P42**

Proclees
A challenge given to one's opponent.
RC: **P43**
Example: Give it your best shot!

Prodiorthosis
The act of preparing one's hearers for something shocking or overwhelming.
RC: **P44**
Example: Horatio here continues after just having told Hamlet that he saw the ghost of Hamlet's father the night before: "Season your admiration for a while With an attent ear, till I may deliver, Upon the witness of these gentlemen, This marvel to you." — Shakespeare, *Hamlet 1.2.189-195*

Proecthesis
When a justification is made in one's conclusion.
RC: **P45**

Progressio
To position several comparisons around a point.
RC: **P46**

Progymnasmata
A set of fundamental exercises meant to prepare rhetoric students for effective communication (specifically oration).

Notes: **Classical Progymnasmata (Exercises):**
1. **Granting Voice** (Fable) – Take a Fable and amplify it – usually done by rewriting specific speeches of the character within to make them more appealing, descriptive, or stronger.
2. **Narrative** – Telling stories or finishing a story that has already been started. A method used today by professional teachers of speech is to assign the reading of children's books aloud – this accomplishes the same results in expression and tone.
3. **Chreia** – A brief talk about a person's character or some notable action or deed.

4. **Refutation** – An oration done in an attempt to discredit a theory or person – the classically famous topic was centered around a myth or legend.

5. **Confirmation** – This exercise is the direct opposite of the Refutation exercise, and therefore would follow after in a debate against the previously supported view.

6. **Commonplace** – much like the previous two exercises except it was argument focused upon a particular moral choice or behavior.

7. **Encomium** – An exercise which gives praise to a person, place, or thing.

8. **Vituperation** – An exercise, opposite to the previous one, which condemns certain evils in a person, place, or thing.

9. **Comparison** – An exercise which gives both sides of an argument or two aspects of a thing and gives qualities of both – in a comparison.

10. **Impersonation** – An exercise where one gives a speech like he was another person – an exercise based on Sermocinatio or Diologismus.

11. **Description** – A description – an attempt to make something visible and strong in the audience's mind.

12. **Thesis/Theme** – A debate type of exercise where an idea is examined – today's research paper.

13. **Court/law** – A kind of thesis/theme exercise in which one examines both sides of a law or infringement thereof.

14. **Enargia** – A general speech of description.

15. **Translation** – Composing a delivering an oration which is in a language unfamiliar to the audience and the speaker.

16. **Prose or Poetry** – Transferring poetry into prose or prose into poetry.

17. **Sentence Varriations** – Adding, subtracting, substituting, and altering both in grammatical structure and rhetorical figure in a given sentence. For example, write the sentence, "your letter delighted me very much," 100 different ways.

Prolepsis

Speaking of something to come as though it had or is occurring – usually to create anticipation.

RC: **P47**

Prosapodosis
Providing, in parallel structure, a reason for each point in a series or divisions of a point.
RC: **P48**
Example: "As I am man, my state is desperate for my master love:
As I am woman (now alas the day)
What trifles sighs shall poor Olivia breathe?
O time, thou must untangle this, not I,
It is too hard a knot for me t'untie." – Shakespeare, *12ᵗʰ Night Act II Scene II*

Notes: Prosapodosis is a specific type of Eutrepismus.

Prolepsis
Pretending to ignore something but stating it outright – usually in some detail.
RC: **P49**

Notes: Prolepsis is a relative of Intimation, Occultatio, and Paralipsis.

Prosopographia
The vivid description of someone's face or character…or a description of mystical or imaginary beings.
RC: **P50**
Example: His cheeks spread away from his nose like two plains of peach and his nose rose as a mountain between, pointed and narrow. The entirety of his face was surrounded on all sides by unkempt hair.

Notes: See Enargia.

Protherapeia
The attempt to prepare one's audience for something to come by using comforting speech.
RC: **P51**
Example: Today, in the place, you may not hear what you expect to hear…

Prothesis
The addition of a letter or syllable to the beginning of a word.

RC: **P52**
Example: Around we went <u>a</u>walking.

Notes: Prothesis is a type of Metaplasm. See Metaplasm.

Protrope
A call to action.
RC: **P53**
Example: Rise and stand up for what you believe in.

Notes: Protrope is a more impersonal form of Optatio. It calls the audience to an aim which is not necessarily shared by the speaker. Optatio, on the other hand, creates a common desire. See Optatio.

Proverb
One of several terms describing short, pithy sayings.
RC: **P54**

Notes: A proverb, more than its relatives, gains its strength from tradition and past experience. See Adage.

Prozeugma
A series of clauses in which the verb employed in the first is understood in the ones to follow.
RC: **P55**
Example: Time or'takes beauty, power grace, and fear reason.

Notes: See Zeugma.

Pysma
The asking of multiple questions successively – usually associated with being overwhelmed by questioning.
RC: **P56**
Example: Did you or did you not take that gold watch? Were you in the house? Were you in the area? Or were you somewhere else? And why didn't you tell us

this was your brother? Or that you even had a brother? Did you take it? Why did you take it?

Notes: Pysma is the strongest Figure of Questioning.

R

Ratiocinatio
Reasoning by asking questions.
RC: **R1**
Example: "What's this, What's this? Is this her fault or mine? The tempter or the tempted who sins most?" – Shakespeare, *Measure for Measure Act II Scene II*

Notes: Ratiocinatio is generally seen as reasoning done, by question, with oneself. See Figures of Questioning.

Rebounde
A synonym of Antanaclasis.

Reciprocatio
A synonym of Antanaclasis.

Recompencer
A synonym of Antanagoge.

Recordatio
A synonym of Anamnesis.

Repotia
A dialogue celebrating a wedding feast.

Restrictio
Making an exception which restricts or limits what has been said.
RC: **R2**
Example: That cake is the best cake I have ever tasted – **in this restaurant**.

Notes: Restrictio is almost identical to Correctio – except it limits the previous statement instead of altering it. See Figures of Definition.

Rhetoric
Rhetoric is the study of effective speaking and writing.

Famous Definitions of Rhetoric
Plato: [Rhetoric] is the "art of enchanting the soul."

Aristotle: "Rhetoric is the faculty of discovering in any particular case all of the available means of persuasion."

Cicero: "Rhetoric is one great art comprised of five lesser arts: inventio, dispositio, elocutio, memoria, and pronunciatio." Rhetoric is "speech designed to persuade."

Quintilian: "Rhetoric is the art of speaking well" or "...good man speaking well."

Francis Bacon: "The duty and office of rhetoric is to apply reason to imagination for the better moving of the will."

George Campbell: "[Rhetoric] is that art or talent by which discourse is adapted to its end. The four ends of discourse are to enlighten the understanding, please the imagination, move the passion, and influence the will."

Henry Ward Beecher: "Not until human nature is other than what it is, will the function of the living voice-the greatest force on earth among men-cease...I advocate, therefore, in its full extent, and for every reason of humanity, of patriotism, and of religion, a more thorough culture of oratory and I define oratory to be the art of influencing conduct with the truth set home by all the resources of the living man."

I. A. Richards: "Rhetoric is the study of misunderstandings and their remedies."

Richard Weaver: That "which creates an informed appetite for the good."

Erika Lindemann: "Rhetoric is a form of reasoning about probabilities, based on assumptions people share as members of a community."

Philip Johnson: "Rhetoric is the art of framing an argument so that it can be appreciated by an audience."

Andrea Lunsford: "Rhetoric is the art, practice, and study of human communication."

Kenneth Burke: "The most characteristic concern of rhetoric [is] the manipulation of men's beliefs for political ends.... the basic function of rhetoric [is] the use of words by human agents to form attitudes or to induce actions in other human agents."

George Kennedy: "Rhetoric in the most general sense may perhaps be identified with the energy inherent in communication: the emotional energy that impels the speaker to speak, the physical energy expanded in the utterance, the energy level coded in the message, and the energy experienced by the recipient in decoding the message."

Lloyd Bitzer: "...rhetoric is a mode of altering reality, not by the direct application of energy to objects, but by the creation of discourse which changes reality through the mediation of thought and action."

Douglas Ehninger: "...that discipline which studies all of the ways in which men may influence each other's thinking and behavior through the strategic use of symbols."

Gerard A. Hauser: "Rhetoric is an instrumental use of language. One person engages another person in an exchange of symbols to accomplish some goal. It is not communication for communication's sake. Rhetoric is communication that attempts to coordinate social action. For this reason, rhetorical communication is explicitly pragmatic. Its goal is to influence human choices on specific matters that require immediate attention."

C. H. Knoblauch: "...rhetoric is the process of using language to organize experience and communicate it to others. It is also the study of how people use language to organize and communicate experience. The word denotes both distinctive human activity and the "science" concerned with understanding that activity."

John Locke: "...that powerful instrument of error and deceit."

Charles Bazerman: "The study of how people use language and other symbols to realize human goals and carry out human activities...ultimately a practical study offering people great control over their symbolic activity."

Michael Hyde and Craig Smith: "The primordial function of rhetoric is to 'make-known' meaning both to oneself and to others. Meaning is derived by a human being in and through the interpretive understanding of reality. Rhetoric is the process of making known that meaning. Is not rhetoric defined as pragmatic communication, more concerned with the contemporary audiences and specific questions than with universal audiences and general questions?"

Alfred North Whitehead: "The creation of the world -- said Plato -- is the victory of persuasion over force. The worth of men consists in their liability to persuasion."

Samuel M. Edelman: "Rhetoric can be defined as the art or method of reconciling...individual and systemic goals and constraints."

Andrew King and Jim Kuypers: "The strategic use of communication, oral or written, to achieve specifiable goals."

Richard E. Vatz: "This [is the] sine qua non of rhetoric: the art of linguistically or symbolically creating salience. After salience is created, the situation must be translated into meaning."

Three Branches of Rhetoric

"Rhetoric falls into three divisions, determined by three classes of listeners to speeches, for of the three elements in speech making — speaker, subject, and person addressed — it is the last one, the hearer, that determines the speech's end and object. The hearer must be either a judge, with a decision to make about things past or future, or an observer. A member of the assembly decides about future events, a juryman about past events: while those who merely decide on the orator's skill are observers. From this is follows that there are three divisions of oratory – (1) Political, (2) Forensic, and (3) Ceremonial oratory of display."[13]

1. **Judicial** (forensic): to accuse or defend.
2. **Deliberative** (legislative): to exhort or dissuade.
3. **Epidictic** (ceremonial or demonstrative): to commemorate or blame.

"These three kinds of rhetoric refer to three different kinds of time. The political orator is concerned with the future...the party in a case at law is concerned with the past...the ceremonial orator is concerned with the present, since all men praise or blame in view of the state of things existing at the time."[14]

"There is little doubt that these categories do not exhaust the kinds of discourse (or even oratory) possible. Quintilian, for example, cataloged many other possible divisions of discourse outlined from antiquity (3.4). Yet these three have persisted and still prove useful in rhetorical analysis, partly because they focus on common social situations where persuasion is important and on broad categories of intention (the purposes listed above)."[15]

Five Canons of Rhetoric
1. **Invention:** Discovering and creating something to say.
2. **Arrangement:** Ordering one's oration or speech.
3. **Style:** Deciding what words and what figures will be used – the composition. The concerns of style: Correctness, Clarity, Propriety, Ornateness, and Evidence.
4. **Memory:** The memorization and human analysis done before one delivers an oration.
5. **Delivery:** The actual giving of an argument, oration, or speech – putting into action all the preparation.

"These categories have served both analytical and generative purposes. That is to say, they provide a template for the criticism of discourse (and orations in particular), and they give a pattern for rhetorical education. Rhetorical treatises through the centuries have been set up in light of these five categories, although memory and delivery consistently have received less attention. Rhetoric

---

[13] Aristotle, *The Art of Rhetoric*. Trans. John Henry Freese. Loeb Classical Library. 1982
[14] Ibid.
[15] Ibid.

shares with another longstanding discipline, dialectic, training in invention and arrangement. When these disciplines competed, rhetoric was sometimes reduced to style alone.

Although the five canons of rhetoric describe areas of attention in rhetorical pedagogy, these should not be taken as the only educational template for the discipline of rhetoric. Treatises on rhetoric also discuss at some length the roots or sources of rhetorical ability, and specific kinds of rhetorical exercises intended to promote linguistic facility."[16]

Other Rhetorical Resources

1. Rhetoric, by Aristotle (355 BC)
2. Ad Herennium, by Cicero (100 BC)
3. De invention, by Cicero (87 BC)
4. De oratore, by Cicero (55 BC)
5. Institutio Oratoria, by Quintilian (95 AD)
6. Longinus (100 AD)
7. De Doctrina Christiana, by Augustine (426 AD)
8. The Marriage of Philology and Mercury, by Martianus Capella (429)
9. De topicis differentiis, by Boethius (524)
10. Disputatio, by Alcuin (800)
11. Ars versificatoria, by Matthew of Vendome (1175)
12. Poetria nova, by Geoffrey of Vinsauf (1210)
13. Forma praedicandi, by Robert de Basevorn (1320)
14. Rhetoricorum libri, by George of Trebizond (1444)
15. De copia, by Erasmus (1510)
16. De ratione studii, by Erasmus (1512)
17. Elements of Rhetoric, by Melanchthon (1521)
18. Arte or Crafte of Rethoryke, by Leonard Cox (1530)
19. A Treatise on Schemes and Tropes, by Richard Sherry (1550)
20. The Arte of Rhetorique, by Thomas Wilson (1553)
21. Dialectique, by Peter Ramus (1555)
22. De arte rhetorica, by Cypriano Soares (1560)
23. The Foundacion of Rhetorike, by Richard Rainolde (1563)
24. Garden of Eloquence, by Henry Peacham (1577)
25. The Arcadian Rhetoricke, by Abraham Fraunce (1588)
26. The Arte of English Poesie, by George Puttenham (1589)

---

[16]   Ibid.

Rhetorical Coding

A method of analysis which breaks orations, informal speeches, and written works down into a system of numbers which correspond to Rhetorical figures and patterns (see *Appendix A*).

Example:

	A20			
A32	B6		B6	E10
A11 – E17 – E39 – A75 – E17- A30 - E8 – R1 – D22 – D8 – E17 – T10 – S25				

Rhetorical Patterns

A combination and mixture of multiple rhetorical devices into one phrase, sentence, or collection of sentences. The most effective communication results from properly built and blended Rhetorical Patterns. In Rhetorical Coding, Rhetorical Patterns are written in vertical stacks.

S

Sarcasmus
Use of mockery, verbal taunts, or bitter Irony.
RC: **S1**

Scesis Onomaton
A sentence or phrase which has words that are identical or similar and are repeated throughout.
RC: **S2**
Example: "Ah, sinful nation,
a people laden with iniquity,
offspring of evildoers,
children who deal corruptly!" – Isaiah 1:4 ESV

Notes: A Figure of Repetition.

Schematismus
Concealing a meaning by using figurative language, either out of necessity or for humor's sake.
RC: **S3**
Example: Anyone could be listening in on this conversation so I must refrain from telling you of the hour that I will arrive. **I will only say that the same hour that you were so forcefully pushed upon me will be the same hour of my arrival.**

Notes: See Enigma, Noema, and Skotison.

Scheme

A creative deviation from the normal arrangement of words.
RC: **S4**
Example: Are you working hard or hardly working?

Notes: Scheme and Trope are closely related. A Trope is a Figure which deviates from the flat meaning or the specific use of a **word** in a sentence – having the idea that it changes or transposes a single entity within. A Scheme is a Figure which deals more with the **arrangement of words** in a sentence – having the idea that it holistically manipulates an entire sentence. See Figures of Speech and Trope.

Sententia

One of several terms describing short, pithy sayings.
RC: **S5**

Notes: See Adage.

Sermocinatio

Speaking dramatically in the first person – as if you were someone else.
RC: **S6**
Example: And the Lord, standing in the midst of pure darkness, said, **"Let there be light!"** and light burst forth.

Notes: Sermocinatio is similar to Dialogismus except it assumes another person's voice in a **dramatic way**. Dialogismus is preferred in more serious circumstances or when the person who is being quoted is one whose voice is more of a distraction than assistance. Sermocinatio is preferred in most occasions, because it seeks to capture not only the content of a specific thought, but it gives it in its proper context, so to speak.

Significatio

To state very little, but to imply a great deal – done by either strong and universal diction or just general emphasis.
RC: **S7**

Notes: Significatio is a relative of Intimation, Occultatio, and Paralipsis.

Simile

An explicit comparison, often (but not necessarily) employing "like" or "as."

RC: **S8**

Example: "Let us go then, you and I,

While the evening is spread out against the sky,

Like a patient etherized upon a table." – T.S. Eliot, *The Love Song of J. Alfred Prufrock*

Notes: Simile is a type of Comparatio which differs from a Metaphor in one great aspect – it makes the comparison very evident. It does not conceal the meaning and carry on but states the comparison directly. See Comparatio.

Skotison

Purposeful obscurity.

RC: **S9**

Solecism

An element of speech or writing that is incorrect grammatically.

RC: **S10**

Soraismus

To mingle different languages affectedly or without skill.

RC: **S11**

Example: "Most barbarous imitation! Yet a kind of insinuation, as it were, in via, in way, of explication; facere, as it were, replication, or rather, ostentare, to show, as it were, his inclination, after his undressed, unpolished, uneducated, unpruned, untrained, or rather, unlettered, or ratherest, unconfirmed fashion, to insert again my haud credo for a deer." – Shakespeare, *Love's Labor Lost Act IV scene ii*

Notes: Soraismus includes devices such as Hebraism and Graecismus.

Sorites

A chain of building claims or reasons.

RC: **S12**

Subjectio
When one questions themselves, and then answers that question, on how an argument should proceed.
RC: **S13**

Notes: A close relative of Hypophora. See Figures of Questioning.

Syllepsis
When a single word, which is modifying or controlling two different words, must be defined or understood differently depending on the word.
RC: **S14**
Example: "We must all hang together or assuredly we will all hang separately." – Benjamin Franklin

Notes: Syllepsis is a type of Zeugma and is often seen as a more ambiguous form. See Zeugma.

Syllogism
A specific and logical argument where a conclusion is drawn from two premises.
RC: **S15**
Example:
1. Major premise = All animals can die.
2. Minor premise = An otter is an animal.
3. Conclusion = Otters can die.

Notes: Aristotle defined a Syllogism in this way: "A discourse in which, certain things having been supposed, something different from the things' supposed results of necessity because these things are so."[17]

General Rules:
1. It must contain only three parts.
2. It must contain only three terms.
3. The middle term must be in one of the premises.
4. A term may not be a part of the conclusion if it was not a part of one of the premises.

---

[17] Aristotle, *The Art of Rhetoric*. Trans. John Henry Freese. Loeb Classical Library. 1982.

5. If one of the premises is negative than the conclusion must also be negative.
6. If there are two negative premises, then no conclusion can be created.
7. If a premise is dependent or incomplete, then a conclusion will be likewise incomplete.
8. If either of the premises are incomplete or dependent, then the conclusion cannot be created.
9. If either or both of the premises are empirical or propositional then the conclusion has to be of the same suit.

Syllogismus

Using a remark or image to call upon the audience to draw an obvious conclusion.
RC: **S16**
Example: We have caught him red-handed!

Notes: Syllogismus is a chain of reasoning that is even shorter than an Ethymeme.

Symperasma

A conclusion that includes a brief summary of former concepts.
RC: **S17**
Notes: Symperasma is from the Greek word meaning, "bring together" and is a more powerful and usually concise version of Conclusio.

Symploce

Beginning a series of lines, clauses, or sentences with the same word or phrase while simultaneously repeating a different word or phrase at the end of each element in this series.
RC: **S18**
Example: When it seems like there is no hope, we continue to hope. When the light fades and the darkness comes, we continue to hope.

Notes: From the Greek, meaning to "interweave" - Symploce is a Figure of Repetition that mixes Anaphora and Epistrophe together. See Figures of Repetition.

Synaeresis
When two syllables are contracted into one.
RC: **S19**
Example: When "New Orleans" is pronounced "Nawlins."

Notes: Synaeresis is the creation of a diphthong and is a kind of Metaplasm. The opposite is done by the figure Diaeresis. Like all other Metaplasms, Synaeresis is best suited to poetry. See Metaplasm.

Synaloepha
The omission of vowels which occur together at the end of one word and the beginning of another.
RC: **S20**
Example: I'll take one; you take *th'other*.

Notes: Synaloepha is a type of Metaplasm.

Synathroesmus
The use of many adjectives or descriptors for the sake of effect – usually used as a means of abuse or attack.
RC: **S21**
Example: The old man was a desperate, ugly, evil, horrible fiend.

Notes: Synathroesmus is a mixture of Synonymia and Congeries.

Synchoresis
Conceding to the judgment of another.
RC: **S22**

Notes: Synchoresis has often been given a definition more like its brother devise, Paromologia, which is the act of giving in to a minor point to win a stronger one. It is also related to Anacoenosis and Epitrope.

Synchysis
The confused arrangement of words in either a sentence or phrase.
RC: **S23**

Notes: Synchysis is seen as the opposite of most figures of composition or style – a vice.

Syncope
Cutting letters or syllables from the middle of a word.
RC: **S24**
Example: When "library" is pronounced "library."

Notes: See Metaplasm.

Syncrisis
Comparison and contrast in parallel clauses.
RC: **S25**
Example: I was worse than a leper, because my desensitization was not of the nerves but of the heart.

Synecdoche
A whole is named or replaced by a part.
RC: **S26**
Example: All **hands**-on deck! (Here the term "hands" is used to call the entire person.)

Notes: Synecdoche is a relative of taxis.

Synesis
Arranging words by their logical connections and not by grammar.
RC: **S27**

Notes: A kind of Anacoluthon.

Syngnome
Forgiveness granted for wrong done.
RC: **S28**

Notes: This device is one which would stand consistent with an appeal to Pathos. If one desires to persuade his audience that he is merciful he must show mercy.

Synoeciosis
A coupling or bringing together of contraries, but not in order to oppose them to one another
RC: **S29**

Synonymia
The use of several synonyms in order to explain or amplify a given point.
RC: **S30**
Example: Oh, to lay hold of what your heart dost seek, oh what **joy**, what **delight**, what **bliss**.

Notes: Synonymia is a specific type of Epanorthosis and Horismus. There are generally two ways to incorporate this figure – either to explain or amplify. One could simple state the primary concept or word and then give, in any amount of detail, the synonyms. This method allows the audience to think about the differences and understand fully the comparisons and contrasts being made. The second method is done in conjunction with Brachylogia – without too much Exergasia or Epanorthosis or with Traductio. This method minimizes the Logos and raises the Pathos. See Figures of Repetition and Figures of Definitions.

Synthesis
A composition that is appropriate sounding.

Syntheton
When two words are joined by a conjunction for emphasis.
RC: **S31**
Example: Have you ever been to Europe: to France, England and Spain, Germany, Poland, and Switzerland?

Notes: Syntheton is only effective when a conjunction is not necessary but used anyway. It is a figure used to emphasize a particular set amongst a list (as in the above example) or two specific traits of an individual without breaking off to give a description. The difference between this device and others related to it (which use conjunctions for emphasis) lies in its attempt to simply emphasize without equality.

Synzeugma
Using a verb to join and thus connect two phrases.
RC: **S32**
Example: With age beauty fades and with sickness also.

Notes: See Zeugma.

Systole
The act of making a long vowel sound short.
RC: **S33**

Notes: Systole is seen as a type of Metaplasm and is considered the opposite of Diastole.

Systrophe
Listing many qualities or descriptions of someone or something.
RC: **S34**
Example: "What [a] piece of work is a
man, how noble in reason, how infinite in faculties, in
form and moving, how express and admirable in
action, how like an angel in apprehension, how like a
god! the beauty of the world; the paragon of animals;
and yet to me what is this quintessence of dust?" — Shakespeare, *Hamlet Act II Scene II*

Notes: Systrophe is famous for its excessive description and absence of definition. A proper Systrophe will emphasize characteristics but not answer any questions about the object or person. It is a relative of Eutrepismus.

T

Tapinosis
Changing a name of something which weakens its dominance or belittles its importance.
RC: **T1**
Example: Said of the Mississippi River: "a stream."

Notes: A kind of Meiosis.

Tasis
Holding out a specific vowel or consonant in the pronunciation of a word or phrase because of its pleasant sound.
RC: **T2**
Example: Some words are abrupt words like, "tree," but then there are those words which, almost by their very nature, must be sustained: like the word "beauteous."

Notes: Tasis is a device mainly found in oratory alone. See Phonoaesthetics.

Tautologia
The vain or wearisome repetition of the same idea in different words – wearisome Exergasia.
RC: **T3**
Example: Oh, what a gross serpent, a cunning wretch, oh what a horrid deceiver are you, you snake of death and anger pent up. You who are self-glorifying and yet unable to satisfy yourself or others, you wretched and malicious being, you dragon of old and of great depths; how you have flown upward to bring us downward. You are certainly horrid and horrid forever.

114

Notes: Although Tautology is usually seen as a Vice it can be useful if controlled properly and used creatively – humorous use or for memorization. Tautology is a Figure of Repetition. See Figures of Repetition.

Taxis

To divide a subject into its various components or attributes.
RC: **T4**
Example: **Starches, carbohydrates,** and **proteins** have become the center of American holidays. (These subordinate components of food have replaced that word.)

Notes: Taxis is a general term which is further put to use by figures such as Synecdoche.

Thaumasmus

To marvel at something rather than to state it in a matter of fact way.
RC: **T5**
Example: "O, Wonder! How many goodly creatures are there here! How beauteous mankind is! O brave new world, that has such people in't" – Shakespeare, *The Tempest, Act V scene i*

Notes: Thaumasmus is one of the most powerful appeals to Pathos in the arsenal of the orator. It also can be a very effective means of Ethos, for it not only drives emotional arousal, but it also shows the audience that you as a speaker really care and feel as they do and have passion in your soul. From experience it is hard to overuse such a device.

Tmesis

Interjecting a word or phrase between parts of a compound word or between syllables of a word.
RC: **T6**

Topographia

A vivid description of a place.
RC: **T7**

Notes: See Enargia.

Topothesia

A vivid description of an imaginary place.
RC: **T8**

Notes: See Enargia.

Traductio

Repeating the same word variously throughout a sentence or thought.
RC: **T9**
Example: People who do nothing more in **life** than to pursue God with their whole **life** will find that their **life** was well spent.

Notes: Traductio is a Figure of Repetition. Although this device can be used in jest, it suits a more serious form of expression. See Figures of Repetition.

Tricolon

Three Parallel elements of the same length occurring together in a series.
RC: **T10**
Example: "Veni, vidi, vici." — Julius Caesar

Notes: Tricolon is usually most effective when the elements become increasingly more powerful. Tricolon is a relative of Hendiatris and Isocolon.

Trivium

A classical curriculum comprised of three subjects: grammar, logic (Dialectic), and Rhetoric.

Notes: The word is a Latin term meaning "the three ways" or "the three roads", forming the foundation of a medieval liberal arts education. "In true liberal education…the essential activity of the student is to relate the facts learned into a unified, organic whole, to assimilate them as… the rose assimilates food from the soil and increases in size, vitality, and beauty."[18] In the Trivium,

---

[18] Joseph, Miriam. *The Trivium: The Liberal Arts of Logic, Grammar, and Rhetoric.* 2002. Paul Dry Books, Inc.

grammar teaches the mechanics of a language; **logic (or Dialectic)** teaches the "mechanics" of thought and analysis; and **Rhetoric** is the use of language to persuade.

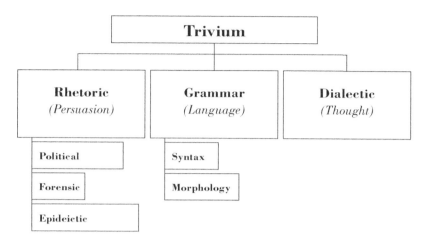

Division of the Language Arts:

Phonetics: Combination of sounds to form words (verbal).

Spelling: Combinations of letters to form words (correctly).

Grammar: Combination of words to form sentences.

Rhetoric: Combination of sentences and paragraphs into a holistic composition that is beautiful, clear, and powerful (and properly so).

Logic (Primarily Dialectic): Composition of thoughts and proofs in such a way to derive truth.

Trope

A deviation, creatively done, from the normal use or relationship of a word.

RC: **T11**

Example: I eat like a **bear**! (A word which means something other than its obvious meaning.)

Notes: Trope and Scheme are closely related. A Trope is a figure which deviates from the flat meaning or the specific use of a word in a sentence – having the idea that it changes or transposes a single entity within. A Scheme is a figure which deals more with the arrangement of words in a sentence – having the idea that it holistically manipulates an entire sentence.

Z

Zeugma
The joining of two or more parts of a sentence with a single common verb or adjective. A Zeugma employs both Ellipsis, the omission of words which are easily understood, and Parallelism, the balance of several words or phrases.
RC: **Z1**
Example: Mr. Benter **bid** for the item and us goodnight.

Notes: **Kinds of Zeugma:**
1. **Diazeugma:** An instance in which a subject governs several verbs or verb phrases.
2. **Epizeugma**: Placing the verb that holds the entire sentence together either at the very beginning or the very ending of that sentence.
3. **Hypozeugma**: A construction of phrases or words of equal strength or importance being placed before the word on which they all rely.
4. **Mesozeugma**: Placing a common verb for many subjects in the middle of a construction.
5. **Prozeugma**: A series of clauses in which the verb employed in the first is implied in the others.
6. **Synzeugma**: Using a verb to join and thus connect two phrases.
7. **Syllepsis:** When a single word, which is modifying or controlling two different words, must be defined or understood differently depending on the word.

Appendix A: List of Most Commonly Used Rhetorical Devices

Accumulatio	A5	Bringing together various points made throughout a speech and presenting them again in a climactic way.
Adhortatio	A11	A commandment, promise, or exhortation intended to move one's consent or desires.
Affirmatio	A16	Stating something as though it had been in dispute or in answer to a question, though it has not been.
Alliteration	A20	Repetition of the same letter or sound within nearby words.
Analogy	A29	A comparison drawn from like figures between two different things.
Anamnesis	A30	Calling to memory past matters. More specifically, citing a past author from memory.
Anaphora	A32	Repetition of the same word or group of words at the beginning of neighboring clauses, sentences, or lines – granting emphasis to a particular phrase or word.
Anesis	A36	Adding a concluding sentence or phrase that diminishes the effect of what has been said previously.
Anthypophora	A41	Reasoning done by asking oneself questions and then immediately answering them.
Apagoresis	A54	A statement designed to inhibit someone's actions or desires.
Apodixis	A61	Proving a statement by referring to common knowledge or general experience.
Aposiopesis	A66	Breaking off suddenly in the middle of speaking, usually with the excuse of being overcome with emotion.
Articulus	A71	Placing phrases or words together without any conjunctions separating them.
Assonance	A74	Repetition of similar vowel sounds, preceded and followed by different consonants, in the stressed syllables of adjacent words.
Assumptio	A75	The introduction of a point to be considered, especially an extraneous argument.
Asyndeton	A78	The omission of conjunctions between clauses, often resulting in a hurried rhythm or vehement effect.
Augendi Causa	A79	Increasing volume or the use of inflection for emphasis.
Auxesis	A80	Arranging words or clauses in a sequence of increasing force.
Battologia	B1	Vain repetition.
Bdelygmia	B3	Expressing hatred and abhorrence of a person, word, or deed.

Braduse	B6	To slow the pace or delivery of one's speech – either to produce an emotional affect or to emphasize a certain point or idea.
Brachylogia	B7	The absence of conjunctions between single words.
Characterismus	C11	The description of a persons' character.
Chorographia	C15	The description of a particular nation.
Commoratio	C24	Dwelling on or returning to one's strongest argument.
Conduplicatio	C30	The repetition of certain words, phrases, or clauses.
Deesis	D3	An expression of desire or need – usually made in conjunction with the name of a deity.
Diacope	D8	Repetition of a word with one or more words between them to express emotion.
Dialogismus	D10	Speaking as something or someone else.
Dialysis	D11	To present alternatives – usually in detail.
Digressio	D19	A departure from logical progression in an oration or informal speech.
Distinctio	D22	Producing clarity by explaining the definition of a term or phrase.
Enargia	E8	A vivid and lively description.
Energia	E10	A general term referring to the energy of an expression.
Epanorthosis	E17	Altering or amending a thought to make it stronger or clearer.
Epicrisis	E22	Quoting a passage – usually to make comment upon it.
Epizeuxis	E34	The repetition of words without any other words in between – mainly for emotional emphasis.
Erotema	E35	To ask a strong question as to affirm or deny something.
Erotesis	E36	A question that does not need or imply a response.
Eucharistia	E38	To give thanks for something received.
Euche	E39	A vow or promise.
Eutrepismus	E43	Numbering and pondering parts or points under consideration.
Excitatio	E45	To keep an audience from boredom by exciting them.
Exergasia	E48	Repetition of the same idea, changing either its wording or delivery.
Exuscitatio	E51	Stirring up one's hearers by expressing personal feelings.
Hebraism	H1	Making use of a Hebrew content or form.
Horismus	H10	A clear and concise definition.
Isocolon	I6	A series of phrases or short clauses which are similarly structured and maintain the same length.
Martyria	M3	Confirming something by referring to personal experience.
Mesodiplosis	M9	Repeating an identical word or a set of words in the middle of neighboring clauses.
Metaphor	M14	A comparison made by referring to one thing as another.
Optatio	O5	Expressing a desire.
Palilogia	P3	Repetition of the same word, with none between, for vehemence.

Parable	P5	The explicit drawing of a parallel between two essentially dissimilar things, especially with a moral or didactic purpose.
Paraenesis	P10	A warning of impending evil.
Paranthesis	P14	Insertion of a qualifying word, clause, or sentence.
Polysydeton	P39	Placing excessive conjunctions between clauses.
Protrope	P52	A call to action.
Pysma	P55	The asking of multiple questions successively – usually associated with being overwhelmed by questioning.
Ratiocinatio	R1	Reasoning by asking questions.
Sermocinatio	S6	Speaking dramatically in the first person – as if you were someone else.
Symperasma	S19	A conclusion that includes a brief summary of former concepts.
Syncrisis	S25	Comparison and contrast in parallel clauses.
Thaumasmus	T5	To marvel at something rather than to state it in a matter of fact way.
Traductio	T9	Repeating the same word variously throughout a sentence or thought.
Tricolon	T10	Three Parallel elements of the same length occurring together in a series.

Appendix B: Rhetorical Device Categories

While Classical Rhetoric does not divide these devices into the following categories, there is value in these lists, which allow you to compare and contrast similar devices.

Figures of Comparison
Allegory: A sustained Metaphor continued through whole sentences or even through a whole discourse.
Comparatio: A comparison.
Metaphor: A comparison made by referring to one thing as another.
Simile: An explicit comparison, often (but not necessarily) employing "like" or "as."

Figures of Conclusion
Accumulatio: Bringing together various points made throughout a speech and presenting them again in a climactic way.
Climax: The point of greatest force – often the point of no return.
Conclusio: The last part of an oration.
Epetasis: A concluding sentence intended to sum up and amplify what has just been said.
Epiphonema: A summary in which the idea that was just presented is summed up in a pithy manner - an ornamental summary.
Proecthesis: When a justification is made in one's conclusion.

Figures of Definition
Correctio: The amending of a term or phrase just employed - redefinition.
Distinctio: Producing clarity by explaining the definition of a term or phrase.
Epanorthosis: Altering or amending a thought to make it stronger or clearer.
Horismus: A clear and concise definition.
Restrictio: Making an exception which restricts or limits what has been said.

Synonymia: The use of several synonyms in order to explain or amplify a given point.

Figures of Description

Anemographia: A good and vivid description of wind – usually in an attempt to create a sense of reality.

Astrothesia: A description of a star or stars.

Characterismus: The description of a person's character.

Chorographia: The description of a particular nation.

Chronographia: Vivid representation of a certain historical or recurring time to create an allusion of reality.

Dendrographia: Vivid description of a tree in order to create a picture of reality.

Ecphrasis: A vivid description as to place an object before the mind's eye.

Effectio: A vivid and usually verbal depiction of someone's body – in great detail.

Ethopoeia: The description and portrayal of a character.

Geographia: Creating an illusion of reality by vividly describing the world.

Hydrographia: A vivid description of water in order to create a sense of reality.

Hypotyposis: A vivid description of a person, scene, action, condition, passion etc. used to create a sense of reality.

Pragmatographia: A vivid description of an action.

Prosopographia: The vivid description of someone's face or character...or a description of mystical or imaginary beings.

Topographia: A vivid description of a place.

Topothesia: A vivid description of an imaginary place.

Figures of Division

Merismus: Dividing of a whole into its parts.

Distributio: Divvying roles or duties up to or of a list of people.

Figures of Metaplasm

Antisthecon: The substitution in the middle of a word - example: "reward" becomes "reword."

Aphaeresis: The omission of a syllable or letter at the beginning of a word - example: "until"
becomes "'til."

Apocope: Omitting a letter or syllable at the end of a word - example: "photography" becomes "photo."

Barbarism: The substitution at the end of a word - example: "Love" becomes "Lerve."

Diaeresis: The logical division of a genus into its species or one syllable into two - example: "co-operate" becomes "cooperate."

Diastole: Taking a vowel sound or syllable and lengthening it out - example: "oooooh yeah!"

Ecthlipsis: The omission of either letters or syllables for the sake of poetic meter - example: "until" becomes "'til."

Epenthesis: The addition of a letter, sound, or syllable to the middle of a word - example: The word "warmth" is said with the stop consonant: "P."

Ellipsis - The omission of a word or phrase which is easily understood in the context.

Metathesis: The switching of two or more letters in a word. (Example: "center" becomes "centre."

Paragoge: The addition of a letter or syllable to the end of a word - example: "sore" becomes "sorel."

Prothesis: The addition of a letter or syllable to the beginning of a word - example: "walking" becomes "awalking."

Synaeresis: When two syllables are contracted into one - example: When "New Orleans" is pronounced "Nawlens."

Syncope: Cutting letters or syllables from the middle of a word - example: "Library" becomes "Library."

Systole: The act of making a long vowel sound short.

Figures of Repetition

Adnominatio: Assigning to a proper name its literal or homophonic meaning.

Alliteration: Repetition of the same letter or sound within nearby words.

Anadiplosis: The repetition of the last word (or phrase) from the previous line, clause, or sentence at the beginning of the next. Often combined with climax.

Anaphora: Repetition of the same word or group of words at the beginning of neighboring clauses, sentences, or lines – granting emphasis to a particular phrase or word.

Antaclasis: The repetition of a word or phrase but the meaning of the word changes the second time it is used.

Antistasis: The repetition of a word in a contrary sense.

Assonance: Repetition of similar vowel sounds, preceded and followed by different consonants, in the stressed syllables of adjacent words.

Coenotes: Repetition of two different phrases: one at the beginning and the other at the end of successive paragraphs.

Conduplicatio: The repetition of certain words, phrases, or clauses.

Consonace: The repetition of consonants in words – usually stressed in the same place.

Commoratio: Dwelling on or returning to one's strongest argument.

Diacope: Repetition of a word with one or more words between them to express emotion.

Diaphora: The repetition of a common name.

Epanodos: Altering or amending a thought to make it stronger or clearer.

Epimone: A figure of repetition in which a plea is made over and over in the same words, or closely related words.

Exergasia: Repetition of the same idea, changing either its wording or delivery.

Epanalepsis: Repeating a phrase with a clause or phrase in between.

Epistrophe: Ending a series of lines, phrases, clauses, or sentences with the same word or words.

Epizeuxis: The repetition of words without any other words in between – mainly for emotional emphasis.

Homiologia: Tedious and frivolous repetition.

Isocolon: A series of phrases or short clauses which are similarly structured and maintain the same length.

Mesarchia: The repetition of the same word or words at the beginning and middle of successive sentences.

Mesodiplosis: Repetition of the same word or words in the middle of successive sentences.

Homoipototon: Repetition of the same consonant in neighboring words.

Paroemion: Excessive Alliteration – almost every word in a sentence or thought is alliterated.

Paromoiosis: Parallelism of sound between the words of adjacent clauses whose lengths are equal or approximate to one another.

Ploce: The repetition of a word for emphasis.

Polyptoton: The repetition of a word by using a non-identical form.

Polysyndeton: Placing excessive conjunctions between clauses.

Palilogia: Repetition of the same word, with none between, for vehemence.

Pleonasmus: Use of redundant words, often to strengthen the thought - repetition that is grammatically unneeded.

Symploce: Beginning a series of lines, clauses, or sentences with the same word or phrase while simultaneously repeating a different word or phrase at the end of each element in this series.

Synonymia: The use of several synonyms in order to explain or amplify a given point.

Tautologia: The vane or wearisome repetition of the same idea in different words – wearisome Exergasia.

Traductio: Repeating the same word variously throughout a sentence or thought.

Figures of Questioning

Anthypophora: Reasoning done by asking oneself questions and then immediately answering them.

Dianoea: The use of animated questions and answers to develop an argument.

Epipelxis: Asking a question in order to chide or express grief.

Erotema: To affirm or deny a point strongly by asking it as a question.

Erotesis: A question that does not need or imply a response.

Pysma: The asking of multiple questions successively.

Ratiocinatio: Reasoning with oneself through questions.

Subjectio: Giving an answer to one's own question regarding how an argument should proceed.

Figures of Zeugma

Diazeugma: An instance in which a subject governs several verbs or verb phrases.

Epizeugma: Placing the verb that holds the entire sentence together either at the very beginning or the very ending of that sentence.

Hypozeugma: A construction of phrases or words of equal strength or importance being placed before the word on which they all rely.

Mesozeugma: Placing a common verb for many subjects in the middle of a construction.

Prozeugma: A series of clauses in which the verb employed in the first is implied in the others.

Synzeugma: Using a verb to join and thus connect two phrases.

Syllepsis: When a single word, which is modifying or controlling two different words, must be defined or understood differently depending on the word.

Made in the USA
Monee, IL
16 February 2024